AF662509

Kailash Satyarthi was born on 11 January 1954 in Vidisha, Madhya Pradesh, India. He did his Bachelor of Engineering degree from Bhopal University (now Barkatullah University), followed by a Postgraduate Diploma in Transformer Design. He has actively spoken out on social issues since his childhood. Over the years, he has led many campaigns against issues such as untouchability and child marriage. Under his leadership, more than 1,50,000 children have been rescued from child labour and slavery since 1981. He has survived several fatal attacks conducting rescue operations.

In 1998, he organized the Global March Against Child Labour, which travelled across 103 countries over a period of six months. The direct result of this march was the International Labour Organization Convention 182 against the Worst Forms of Child Labour, which is the only universally ratified convention of the ILO.

To ensure access to education for every child in the world, Satyarthi set up the Global Campaign for Education in 1999. In India, he led a nationwide march to fight for the right to education for all children, which led to an amendment to the Constitution of India to make education a fundamental right. In 2017, he led another Bharat Yatra, a nationwide march covering 11,000 kilometres against sexual abuse and trafficking of children. Soon after the march, a stringent legal framework against sexual abuse of children in India was introduced. He has organized several other campaign marches against child labour and trafficking in India and other parts of South Asia. For the rehabilitation, education and leadership development of survivors, he has established Mukti Ashram, Bal Ashram and Balika Ashram.

For his extraordinary contribution towards the upliftment of humanity, Satyarthi has been awarded the Nobel Peace Prize (2014), the Medal of the Italian Senate, the Parliamentarians for Global Action (PGA) Defender of Democracy Award, the Robert F. Kennedy Human Rights Award, the Harvard Humanitarian Award and the Friedrich Ebert Stiftung Human Rights Award, among others. He has also been awarded honorary doctorates by many reputable universities.

He has more than six publications to his name.

'Why Didn't You Come Sooner?'

Compassion in Action

Stories of Children Rescued from Slavery

KAILASH SATYARTHI

SPEAKING TIGER

SPEAKING TIGER BOOKS LLP
125A, Ground Floor, Shahpur Jat, near Asiad Village,
New Delhi 110049

First published in Hindi by Rajkamal Prakashan in 2022
This English edition published by Speaking Tiger in 2023

Copyright © Kailash Satyarthi 2023

ISBN: 978-93-5447-595-5
eISBN: 978-93-5447-596-2

10 9 8 7 6 5 4 3 2 1

Typeset in Garamond Premier Pro by SÜRYA, New Delhi
Printed at Chaman Enterprises, New Delhi

All rights reserved.
No part of this publication may be reproduced, transmitted, or stored in a retrieval system, in any form or by any means, electronic, mechanical, photocopying, recording or otherwise, without the prior permission of the publisher.

This book is sold subject to the condition that it shall not, by way of trade or otherwise, be lent, resold, hired out, or otherwise circulated, without the publisher's prior consent, in any form of binding or cover other than that in which it is published.

Contents

Author's Note

It has taken me about twelve years to write this book. These stories, forever etched in my mind, however, have been waiting to be told for much longer. This book is a record of the lives of a select few children whose suffering became the fire that melted away the chains of millions of others trapped in slavery. The resilience and courage of these children have added a new chapter to the history of civilization's onward march to freedom. For this reason, what is written on the pages of this book is not mere words. These are voices that have risen from the depths of silence, faces that have emerged from total obscurity and the many hues of a rainbow that have broken through the darkest clouds. Having lived these children's stories with them, their voices and faces have become an indelible part of me too.

Every story you read here will deepen your faith in the triumph of light over darkness, hope over despair, justice over exploitation, compassion over cruelty and humanity over all else. The path to this triumph, however, has been long and difficult. The children in these stories and I have walked together through pain, doubt, fear and danger for many years. And so, despite the anxiety and agitation, these stories also speak to my hopes, dreams and convictions as their fellow traveller. These children have grown up before my eyes, and I have been privy to their inner transformations as their companion. I cannot say for sure what thousands of children like them have learnt from me, but what I have gained from them is invaluable. They immediately found and befriended the child within me and bestowed on me the gift of keeping that child alive and happy. I hope I have been able to do justice to the lives and stories of my young friends in this book.

I have chosen twelve stories that show how various industries—stone quarrying and mica mining, brick kilns, carpet weaving, circuses or even agriculture—can turn children into slaves. These accounts demonstrate how children are trafficked and exploited, physically and sexually abused, forced into child marriage, or beggary or domestic labour.

One of the stories featured in this book is about a girl named Sabo who was freed from a brick kiln in 1981. She became the spark that led to our worldwide movement to end child labour and slavery. On a more personal level, it was the incident that shaped my life's purpose and gave me a direction. Another story is that of Bhavna, who was raped and exploited every day for years in a circus, and had come to despise the sight of men. Her rage was palpable and it took the form of the first proper legal framework against human trafficking in India. Forced to weave intricate carpets with his tiny hands, Kalu's story captures his deep anguish and his equally strong faith in humanity. His slave master, instead of rubbing ointment on his wounds, would cauterize them by stuffing them with phosphorus scraped off from matchsticks and lighting it on fire. Kalu carried the fire from those wounds inside him after he was freed, till he was able to look the President of the United States in the eye and ask him, 'There are more than 250 million children across the world who are still exploited as child labourers... Please tell me, what are you doing for them?'

Another story I've shared here is that of Pradeep, who was

labelled a bad omen not just for his own family but for the whole village. Offered up as sacrifice at the altar of superstition and blind custom, he narrowly escaped death. Having survived unimaginable trauma, today, he is self-reliant and financially independent.

Serving a senior IAS officer day and night, little Ashraf was branded a thief for taking a sip of some leftover milk. The bribe of thousands of rupees offered to them failed to blunt Ashraf's will to fight or rob his mother, Phool Jahan, of her dignity. It was their grit and sacrifice that planted the seed for India's law against domestic child labour.

Then there is the story of Devli, an eight-year-old girl, the third generation of a family trapped in slavery and bonded labour at a stone quarry. After she was freed, she lived in our rehabilitation centres for a few years and vowed to not only end child labour in her village but also ensure that no child is denied an education. In 2008, she would address the United Nations and call upon world leaders to take concrete action to ensure the freedom and education of children. The immediate result of her invocation is for all to see in the following pages. A question Devli asked me as we made our way back after their rescue has stayed with me all these years. Sitting next to me in the car with other children, she said in a bold voice, but one that also betrayed her anger and pain, 'Why didn't you come sooner?'

The lives of none of these children would have been what they are today without Sumedha ji. She was their mother, friend and guide every step of the way. Our own children—Bhuwan and Asmita—have spent the greater part of their childhood with many of these rescued children. From freeing the children to raising them, instilling hope and encouraging their dreams, educating them and helping them become good human beings, our comrade Ramashankar Chaurasia and innumerable companions from Bachpan Bachao Andolan have all been a part of this journey. Our Bal Ashram and Mukti Ashram teachers, mentors and activists have helped build the futures of thousands of children from the ruins of their past.

To protect the privacy of some of these children, their names have been changed in this book. But beyond that, I have tried my best to neither exaggerate any aspect of their stories or to fictionalize these accounts with guesswork. There is nothing more powerful and impactful than the truth itself.

Separating myself from the emotions intertwined with these experiences has proven to be an immense challenge, and weaving them into the narratives presented an even more formidable hurdle. But I am still choosing to undertake this audacious task, fuelled by faith in the compassion of my reader. I know that compassion isn't a weak sentiment. It involves experiencing the pain of others as if it were our own and being strongly driven to alleviate it. It thus represents the most potent approach to selfless problem-solving for both individuals and the world. I hope that this book will play its part in awakening that innate capacity for compassion in everyone who reads it.

'Why Was I Punished for God's Mistake?'

Layers of blind faith have settled upon our minds and consciousness, sometimes in the name of religion and God, sometimes in the garb of tradition and culture, and at yet others, on the pretext of protecting our identity and pride. Gradually, over the centuries, they have solidified, creating divisions within and between us, making us weak, selfish, hateful and violent. This is a story of a venom so powerful that it poisoned even the nectar of a mother's love. It is the story of Pradeep.

It must have been four or five in the evening one day in the scorching summer month of July in 2000. I was sitting in the gol kutiya (round hut) of Bal Ashram along with my wife Sumedha ji and a few children. Bal Ashram is a centre for the education, training and rehabilitation of rescued bonded and child labourers. It is situated near a small town amidst the Aravalli Hills called Viratnagar in Jaipur district, Rajasthan. It had rained in the morning, making the day more pleasant than it would otherwise be. There is something unique about the wild plants that grow here. The hills appear dark and barren during the hot months of May and June, but it takes just a few showers to transform them into a lush green and magnificent sight.

The Ashram is spread across four or five acres. In those days, however, a mere twentieth of the area had any sort of construction. And these were temporary structures for the residence, dining, schooling and training of the children and for the rest of us. The remaining area was an open, rugged field where we had planted some trees and plants. We were discussing ideas for planting more trees there when we saw Hariram, an activist of the Bachpan Bachao Andolan, walking slowly into the Ashram holding a child's hand. The child stumbled as he tried to walk. This wasn't unusual. Children freed from slavery have, more often than not, faced some form of violence and abuse. The children sitting with us had themselves been rescued from slavery. We presumed he was stumbling because he was hurt.

The distance from the round hut to the main entrance to the Ashram was about a hundred metres, and so we ran to the gate and brought the child to the hut. His head was covered in bandages. We wanted to know what had happened. He was injured, shaken and scared, and I felt that he wouldn't want to speak freely among so many people. So I asked the others to leave. Only Hariram and the child were to sit with me. He did not look older than five or six and was wearing a pair of torn khaki shorts and a blue vest. His clothes were soiled and his skinny limbs too appeared to not have been washed for months. His uncut and unkempt hair gave off a strong stench. But the smell could also possibly have been of the festering injuries under the bandages.

I called for chai and biscuits for the two of them. Then, calmly, I sat next to the boy, caressed his hands and placed them between mine. Every now and then, he would pull out one hand from my grasp to scratch his head. I asked him his name, but he just sat silently with his head lowered. I repeated the question several times. He said nothing.

'Bhai Sahab ji, his name is Pradeep,' Hariram intervened. 'Gunjal ji has sent him here,' he said, referring to Rajendra Gunjal, an active member of the Bachpan Bachao Andolan and a socially conscious journalist from Ajmer, Rajasthan.

He continued, 'Gunjal ji saw him working at a chai stall outside a government hospital one day. When he saw the injury on Pradeep's head, he questioned the owner of the stall. The owner told him that the boy had been admitted in the hospital for weeks, unaccompanied. Some people, he didn't know who, had dropped him off at the entrance to the hospital and left immediately. He lay there unconscious till someone took him to the doctor to be treated. The top half of the back of his head was almost entirely sliced. There were no injuries anywhere else on the body.'

'But one has to file a police complaint in cases like these,' I said to Hariram.

'I don't know,' he replied. 'Gunjal ji asked me to bring him to Bal Ashram.'

I went into the Ashram office and immediately dialled Gunjal ji's number.

'As far as I know,' he explained, 'either this case was not referred to the police at all or the police didn't investigate it. Pradeep's life was saved thanks to the care and effort of a few doctors. But as he recovered, the hospital administration was left to decide where to send him. They realized that if he was handed over to the police, it might make things worse.

'There was a tiny chai stall outside the hospital,' Gunjal ji continued, 'which used to cater to the hospital staff. The hospital is relatively small, so the owner of the stall had seen Pradeep several times. He felt sorry for the boy took him in once he was discharged. He convinced the hospital administration to let him keep the boy; he could earn some money by washing utensils and serving the customers. They agreed. I happened to pass by the hospital one day and noticed the owner making him work as a child labourer. He finally recounted this story to me when I insisted on knowing who the boy was.'

Gunjal ji told the owner that while he had shown mercy by keeping the child with him, child labour was a criminal offence. Eventually, he agreed to let Pradeep go.

Even back then, there were innumerable children at the Ashram, such as Deepak, Bhadram and Bhupati, who had little or no memory of their parents. They belonged to different parts of the country and it was impossible to look for their family with the limited information we had about them. Gunjal ji was a journalist. So I requested him to probe deeper into the case with the police and the hospital. Maybe that could help us trace Pradeep's parents.

After the conversation with Gunjal ji, Sumedha ji and I sat

next to Pradeep. Once again, I tried placing his hands between mine but he immediately pulled his hands away. This time, I noticed that his face betrayed a hint of not just mistrust but also fear. I had initially thought that the injury and the resulting trauma had likely caused Pradeep to lose his memory. But now it seemed like he was hiding something on purpose. We never hurry or goad rescued children to tell us about themselves. The terrifying circumstances that they've escaped have made them lose faith in others. It isn't often that they meet people who extend them a helping hand. Since they've never been respected, they in turn find it difficult to develop feelings of love or respect for others.

Sumedha ji fed him sweets and candies with her hands. After some initial hesitation, he ate them, but there was no emotion on his face. Later, we called a few other children to come over and meet him. The evening was drawing to a close and it would have been difficult to take him to the doctor. But since the bandages on his head were already loose and dirty, he allowed us to change them. The wound was still fresh. We cleaned it up and wrapped it in new bandages.

Many challenges lay before us, the first being his medical treatment. The second, of helping him overcome the trauma and apprehension so he could open up and mingle with the other children. Of course, we also needed to find out more about the cause of his injury, and his family.

We asked the principal teacher of the Ashram, Ramkripal Guruji, and two children to accompany Pradeep to the hostel. They helped him bathe and change into clean clothes, and came back with him around dinnertime. He sat with the other children. There were approximately seventy children in the Ashram at the time. We would spread mats on the floor and eat together sitting in two rows facing each other. Sumedha ji and I sat diagonally opposite Pradeep, but we kept a close eye on him. His gaze would shift between us and his brand-new clothes. Still, there was no expression on his face. As we finished eating and proceeded towards our room, I told Pradeep, 'Oh, you look like a hero!' He didn't react, but only stood there looking at us while the teachers and the children walked away.

He was scared, but at that moment we saw a glimmer of belief in his eyes. Instead of sending him to the hostel, we let him stay with Ramkripal Guruji and his family for the night. He woke up late the next morning. It was possibly for the first time in many years that he had slept in peace. We took him to a good doctor nearby in Viratnagar who began his treatment. The doctor believed that the top of Pradeep's head had been struck with a sickle, sword or some other sharp-edged tool, which had caused the severe laceration.

A few days later, on 15 August, we celebrated Independence Day in the Ashram. We celebrate Independence Day and Republic Day with great enthusiasm. The children prepare excitedly for the flag hoisting ceremony by organizing a parade, patriotic songs and dramas. That day, Sumedha ji noticed Pradeep watching the parade carefully and trying to hum something. She called him to sit next to her and started teaching him a popular children's song: '*Nanha munna rahi hoon / Desh ka sipahi hoon / Bolo mere sang / Jai Hind, Jai Hind, Jai Hind.*' (I am a little traveller / A soldier of my country / Come sing with me—Long live India!) He followed her instructions diligently. She bought him a little army costume which he wore on every occasion for several months. Thus began Pradeep's journey of healing.

The children who come to Bal Ashram, Balika Ashram or Mukti Ashram don't know their birthdays. To help them develop a sense of dignity, and an identity of their own, we came up with a novel solution. We decided to pick holidays to celebrate each child's birthday. On that day, the 'birthday boy/girl' is dressed in new clothes and there are festivities all day. Blessings and flowers are showered on him/her. Everyone at the Ashram celebrates by singing, dancing and eating sweets.

We celebrated Pradeep's birthday with great display on one such day. He began the day by joining Sumedha ji and me for the morning prayer ceremonies and then spent the rest of his day having fun with the other children, teachers and activists. The happy little boy was a sight to behold! He went around hopping from the pantry to the office to the hostel to invite people as an excuse to meet them. Through the prayers and festivities, I was trying to read Pradeep and his emotions. I had never seen such a twinkle in his eyes. His full-toothed smile did not fade for a minute!

'I can't believe my birthday is being celebrated like this!' he said to me, hardly able to speak from the excitement.

That day, it felt like a new Pradeep was born. Yet he had not developed love for and faith in others, and neither had he started to form real friendships at the Ashram.

For the past few months, a ten- or eleven-year-old boy named Deepak had been living with us. A day or two after Pradeep's birthday was celebrated, he was seen mingling and chatting with Deepak. Their temperaments were similar. Deepak's behaviour too was reflective of fear, anger and mistrust. The two remained distant from the rest of the children and teachers. Deepak used to hide from the others and trample on flowers and plants ever since he came to the Ashram. Now, both he and Pradeep did it together. Pradeep secretly kept small rocks with him, and would bring down electric bulbs by throwing these at them. He would leave behind food on his dinner plate on purpose. And in the mornings, he would waste several buckets of water while bathing. The children and staff at Bal Ashram never pluck flowers or leaves, and they never waste a morsel of food or a drop of water. Nobody needs to keep an eye on them. Everyone understands the value of these habits and follows them as a way of life.

We didn't know anything about Deepak's family. One of our activists had rescued him from the railway station in Delhi. He had stepped out of a train and was found running between the tracks to escape the police. When the officer caught hold of him he started beating him up. Fortunately, our activist, Rambahadur ji, happened to be present there. He saw what was happening and rushed to stop it. The officer accused Deepak of pickpocketing and was questioning him. But Rambahadur ji convinced the officer to let him go when no wallet or money was found on him. He persuaded Deepak and brought him to Bal Ashram. However, it was very difficult to get Deepak to stay. He had never been to a prison or lock-up. For him, even the Ashram was a prison. Within a week, he scaled the wall and escaped but came back in two days of his own accord.

A few days passed and Deepak began to trust some of the staff at the Ashram. He confided in them that he worked for a group of people who forced children to beg inside trains. They took all the money for themselves and kept the children locked up in a place near Agra. After some time they began to make him pick pockets as well. He was actually trained for it. They handed him a few coins from the loot every day. For every two or three such children, one gang member would keep watch.

Soon, they involved Deepak in another operation. This became his main job.

'They would shove a bunch of old, crumpled clothes in a bag and hide small packets of some substance inside them. Whenever we were sent to beg or steal, we would be made to board the trains without tickets. But when they sent us with these bags, we were always sent with tickets.'

Obviously, the children were being used as drug mules, discreetly transferring contraband substances from one place to another.

'We were given some money for petty expenses,' Deepak told us. 'From that, we saved enough for bidis and cinema tickets.'

One day, Deepak confided in one of the boys at the Ashram, 'Brother, something is worrying me. This man [Kailash Satyarthi] and his wife aren't making us earn and bring back money for them, and they aren't making us work. They don't make us give them massages. They wash their own plates. They try to win our trust by playing and dancing with us. I think that one of these days, they will cleverly steal my kidneys and sell them!'

The boy laughed and responded, 'See, brother, I have been living here for about three years. My kidneys are intact!'

Deepak gave him a tight slap. 'What do *you* know? In the middle of the night, they inject you with something to make you unconscious and then steal your kidneys. That's why you're so thin and weak.'

The boy informed a teacher about the incident, who tried to talk to Deepak about it. But he pushed him away, yelling, 'We know that you all run a kidney-selling racket!'

Some of the words Deepak used were Odia. Another boy, Bhadram, came from the border areas of Andhra Pradesh. We knew that because of the folk songs he used to hum. Bhupati used to speak Tamil slang while a young boy named Vishal spoke the dialect of an area around Bikaner, Rajasthan. All of them were trafficked at a very young age. None of them knew where home was. Apart from making attempts to trace their families themselves, Bal Ashram staff would share all such information with the police as well, and did so for Deepak too.

Pradeep had now been added to this list. He and Deepak became good friends, pugnacious as they both were. Pradeep had the bad habit of eating sand and chewing on rocks. There was little improvement despite psychiatric treatment. Kanhaiya Guruji, a teacher visiting the Ashram, was assigned the special responsibility of keeping an eye on him. But the day Kanhaiya Guruji admonished him for eating sand, Pradeep would make it a point to be even more trouble. He would lightly slap him and run away, shouting, 'Guruji, give me a candy!'

I was on my walk one early winter morning and happened to stop by the terrace of the children's hostel. Pradeep was sitting in a corner. He was holding a pair of scissors, trying to cut through his sweater. Startled to see me there, he threw the sweater on the ground and ran to the exit. But he banged against a door as he tried to escape and fell. I helped him get up and comforted him. Fortunately, he wasn't injured apart from a few minor scratches on his arms. I promptly put my jacket on him, took his sweater and walked away. During lunch later that afternoon, Pradeep saw that I was wearing his sweater, all stitched up. Even though he was a tall kid, the sweater did not fit me. Pradeep walked up to me, grabbed me and started crying. He returned my jacket to me and took his sweater back. A new sweater was given to him, but he continued to wear the stitched sweater for several days.

Every evening, we organized an entertainment programme in the Ashram. We enjoyed ourselves, singing and dancing together. There would also be performances of folk songs and drama. The entertainment served as a form of therapy. But it was more than that. It was a chance to get to know one another, to help the children develop faith in one another and in themselves.

Gradually, we started seeing significant changes in Pradeep. During lunch or the cultural programmes in the evening, he would find a place to sit close to Sumedha ji. While Deepak was talkative, Pradeep was introverted. When spoken to, he only gave short responses. He was the same way even with me.

But something happened one night as we were having our usual cultural event in the Ashram. I had been down with fever and cough for the past day or two. So I sat on the floor next to the children with a woollen blanket wrapped around myself. They would come running to me, and touch my hands and forehead to check if I was still feverish. Pradeep was sitting at a distance from me, next to Sumedha ji. The programme went on. A few children were on the stage telling jokes. The rest of them were rolling on the floor laughing. In the midst of the laughter, Pradeep suddenly burst into tears, sobbing inconsolably. This shocked everyone. For one, the environment was one of fun and frolic, and second, nobody had ever seen Pradeep cry in this manner.

After some pacifying by Sumedha ji, he said, 'Bhai Sahab is ill. Now he will die. What will happen to me now? I don't have anyone else.' This unexpected emotional outburst left Sumedha ji somewhat stunned. Her eyes welled up. Soon, the other children turned to look at them, bringing the programme on the stage to a stop. I thought Pradeep was feeling unwell so I walked up to him and Sumedha ji. When she told me what he had just said, I couldn't hold back my tears either. I held Pradeep close and hugged him. That this boy, distant and always silent, loved me this much left me surprised.

'Dear child, this is just a case of flu because of the changing weather,' I said to him. 'Nobody dies of the flu.'

After much consolation, he quietened down. He smiled at me, but I felt he was putting up a front. His eyes were still moist and he seemed scared. While I hadn't heard Pradeep's words myself, the few sentences that Sumedha ji and the other children relayed back to me made me feel a deep sense of fulfilment about my life and mission. When you witness humanity and childhood re-emerge in a child, it feels like the universe is celebrating. The world seems like a brighter, more hopeful place. That is the miracle of a childhood reclaimed.

The next day, Pradeep was among the first few children to get ready and join the morning prayers and exercises. Everyone was pleasantly surprised by the sudden change in his behaviour. I had stayed up late the previous night thinking about Pradeep, but had not imagined this. He was truly a different person. He had begun to mingle and chat with the others. Every now and then he would bring some complaint from one of the other children to Sumedha ji and use it as an excuse to talk to her.

Pradeep then started to learn to read. One day, he put on a school uniform, walked up to the manager of the Ashram and declared, 'I am also going to school!' Everyone burst out laughing as he stood there wearing a long, loose set of pants tied together by ropes, and an oversized shirt forcefully tucked into his pants. He had stolen an older boy's uniform early that morning. This was how Pradeep expressed his desire to go to school.

Some time after, a remarkable thing happened. Kanhaiya Guruji was getting a haircut one morning when the barber, in an attempt to hurry up, made a slight mistake. Pradeep was sitting close by.

'Guruji, my nana [maternal grandfather] could give you a better haircut!' he exclaimed.

Immediately, Kanhaiya Guruji requested the barber to stop and asked Pradeep to come sit in front of him. He then called Ramkripal Guruji to join them. Both Kanhaiya and Ramkripal had been freed from bonded labour many years ago. They engaged Pradeep in casual conversation and found out that he belonged to a family of barbers, members of a Hindu caste that traditionally acted—and still do in many parts—as messengers of good and bad news in a village. They often use the surname 'Sen' in northern India.

Pradeep remembered that his family members too suffixed 'Sen' to their names. Then on, he got so attached to his surname that he would go around identifying himself as Pradeep Sen, even though children only use their first name in the Ashram. In South Asia, people's surnames are generally a marker of the caste group they are born into, and while these caste-defined surnames can give individuals a sense of belonging to a community, of social and emotional security, they also perpetuate rigidity and intergenerational exploitation and discrimination.

Within a couple of days, Pradeep had started fiddling around with a pair of scissors too. One day, he ran them through the hair of a child named Amarlal, wiping out a good chunk of it. Annoyed by the mockery he was subjected to at the hands of the other children and their amusement at Pradeep's mischief, Amarlal went and beat them up. We had to call the barber from the village nearby to shave off Amarlal's hair entirely. The poor boy had to walk around with a bald head for several weeks.

A few months after this incident, Pradeep convinced his new friend Bunty to avail his services. The hapless Bunty was unaware of the incident with Amarlal. He had seen a movie a few days earlier where the 'hero' had a fancy hairstyle and wanted one just like it for himself. He asked Pradeep to leave the hair at the top and about the crown intact and to shave it off on the sides. Pradeep stood prepared with his razorblade. He first cleaned off the hair on the left and then on the right. But he went beyond the ideal point on the right and, to make up for the error, he came back round to the left to balance it out. The same thing was repeated on the other side, and then again on the left, and so on, but he never seemed satisfied with the results. Bunty's hair now looked like a donkey's mane. This in addition to the several cuts Pradeep's blade had left on his scalp. We had no choice but to get his head shaved off as well.

Sumedha ji used to often travel from Delhi to Bal Ashram. She would stay there for days at a time. I too would join her when I could. One day, Pradeep described to us the landscape around his village. He never spoke about his parents, even to us. Judging from his behaviour, we guessed that he probably had a stepparent whose cruelty he had run away from. He had likely run into an accident or been assaulted by someone to his head after he escaped. With the bits of information they had, including descriptions of his village, our activists got busy looking for Pradeep's family. A few villages near the city of Ajmer looked like they came close. Then, finally, after days of searching, they came across a village and a family of barbers that matched Pradeep's description perfectly. Still, they weren't entirely sure.

A teacher from the village, on the promise of anonymity, informed the activists that there was a family of barbers in the village whose son had gone missing all of a sudden a few years ago. However, when approached, this family denied association with any missing child. The activists showed them a photo of Pradeep, but they didn't recognize him. In the meantime, people from neighbouring homes had begun to assemble. The crowd was angry and vehement in their assertion that no child from their village had ever gone missing. They even accused our activists of belonging to a child kidnapping gang.

While our activists managed to save themselves and escape the crowd, the family and villagers' behaviour had sown seeds of suspicion in their minds. After an adequately long interval, they resumed their investigation, more discreetly this time.

The information that came to light was horrifying. Pradeep did belong to that village, and the said family was indeed his. A few days after he was born, an exorcist had come to the village. He had told the parents of the newborn that they were housing a cursed child. It so happened that later that year the village suffered a drought. Not long after, most likely a knock-on effect of the drought, several people died from a mysterious illness. Pradeep's mother too fell seriously ill. The exorcist stood vindicated that Pradeep was in fact a bad omen. His family and the entire village now declared Pradeep to be so and he was mercilessly scorned. The residents of the village avoided even laying eyes on the so-called cursed child's face. Troubles continued to befall his family, and Pradeep was reflexively blamed for them. Thus brought up with hate and contempt, Pradeep grew to be six years old.

At this time, another exorcist visited the village who proposed a 'solution' to Pradeep's parents and relatives. He claimed that it could release the family from the curse of the child, that it would please Chandi Maa, the demon-slaying form of Shakti, the Hindu goddess of Power, and return the family to a state of well-being. The solution he proposed was to sacrifice the child at the midnight hour of Durga Ashtami (the eighth day of the nine-day festival to worship the nine forms of the goddess Durga). The family agreed.

Every religion grants children a place of respect. No scripture allows the torture of children. On the contrary, they mandate their protection, nurture and education. But afflicted by blatant self-regard, ignorance, dogma or violence, people can find legitimacy even in religion and tradition for their acts of exploitation of children. Even today, intercourse with unmarried young girls is believed to be a way to prolong the life of men. Making young girls of pre-menstrual age plough the fields instead of oxen is believed to yield a better crop. Child marriage, cruelty to child widows, offering of little girls to lifelong service at temples, genital mutilation, throwing six-month-old girls off the terraces of temples, dipping babies in hot oil, child sexual abuse and other such hateful acts remain rampant in out 'places of worship'. Thousands of children are victimized at temples, churches and madrasas. Human sacrifice, particularly that of children, is the nadir of all religious dogma. Justified in the name of God, stories of this disgraceful practice continue to appear in the media every now and then.

The day and time for Pradeep's sacrifice was fixed, and the family made all the arrangements for it. The exorcist and executioner arrived early on that day at the temple located on the adjacent hill. Once Pradeep had fallen asleep, he was carried to the temple and laid facing down. They then proceeded with the rituals that led up to the moment of sacrifice, when the child's head was to be sliced off and placed at the feet of Chandi Maa. But as soon as the executioner raised his weapon to make the final swing, Pradeep woke up and raised his head. As the blade dropped, instead of landing on and slicing his neck, it slashed the top of his head. This was how Pradeep got that severe wound which was covered with bandages when he came to us. They were indignant that Chandi Maa had refused their sacrifice, blaming even this on the child.

Fortunately, however, they took the little boy for dead. And to remove the evidence, they tied up his body in a large jute bag and threw it in the wild. The next day, a man who was on his way for his early morning toilet came across the jute bag with blood trickling from it. Word spread and slowly a crowd began to gather. They examined the bag, moving it back and forth, and began to suspect that there was a human body inside it. When they untied it, they found a child's body soaked in blood. A man noticed that he was still breathing and rushed him to the hospital close by. But with limited treatment available there, some good people dropped him off outside the district hospital in Ajmer. They perhaps wanted to avoid getting caught up in a police investigation.

As shaken as all of us at the Ashram were, we were just as perplexed. We had never come across such a story. The signs of trauma from living through years of contempt and humiliation had been there for us to see. But the story of human sacrifice was beyond our wildest imagination. It was clear to us now why Pradeep had such deep hatred for his parents, and why he mistrusted everyone around him. For that very reason, we held this information back from him.

Whenever anyone asked Pradeep about the injury on his head, he would either remain silent or run away in anger. Sometimes, he would ask his teachers how they thought his head was hurt so badly. He did confide once in the in-house psychologist of the Ashram that his parents had thrown him out of the house, but that was about it. After we had found out about his family, I spent the next couple of days in long conversations with him. We needed to make sure he was mentally prepared for the news.

'If we find your parents,' I asked him after we had been talking a few days, 'what will you do?'

He said nothing at first. After some time, he said, 'It's not possible.'

I asked him why.

After some prodding, he replied, 'They are dead. I stayed with my grandfather.'

I asked him if he knew for certain that they were dead.

'I don't remember,' he responded, 'I was very young at the time.'

I knew how well he lied. A few days later, he told the psychologist that he had lied to me. She found the right moment, and told him the story of the human sacrifice. He showed no sign of sadness, anger or shock as he listened to this horrific story.

'They have always wanted me dead,' he retorted. 'My mother and father would yell at me at every chance they got. They would only give me leftover food. Once, my father got injured and everyone blamed me, when I wasn't even there at the time. One day the neighbour had got a new cow, which died the day after.

Everyone got together and declared that I had cast my sight on the cow as it was coming in, which is why she died. My mother mercilessly beat me up for it. I would sit in the corner of the house and cry all day long. My elder sister used to comfort me when no one was looking and share her candies with me. She only told me that I was a curse who caused everyone harm. I didn't understand it then. Now, after what you have told me, I understand.'

Saying this, he ran out of the room. After hours of nobody seeing him, a search began. Pradeep was found sitting alone on the terrace above the kitchen. The two Gurujis spoke to him and brought him down. He told them that for the two or three years he had been in the Ashram, his biggest fear had been that Sumedha ji and I too would begin hating him if we found out he had a curse upon him. He used to stay away from the clever children in the Ashram, and remained suspicious of them. He feared they might figure out that he was cursed. Whenever a child fell ill, got hurt, or even when the cow in the Ashram died, he would shrink with dread. Within a few hours, he would start breaking things and getting into fights.

He came to me one day. There were many questions in his mind. Everyone knew of his story by now. But this innocent little boy was desperate for answers.

'Bhai Sahab ji,' he began, 'when I was born everyone believed that I was responsible for bringing troubles to my family. But when I was so little, how could I cause those troubles? If I was cursed, why did God create me at all? That means that the mistake lies with the God who created me. So why was I punished for God's mistake?'

He would often ask me, 'I look like other children, so how can I be evil?' I sympathized with him. I didn't lack the words to answer his questions, but I did not have the power to erase his memories. Sumedha ji, the psychologist and I would speak to him at length, and the effects of our talks would last for a few days, but soon enough he would find himself thinking those same thoughts again.

It was during that time that I received news that I was being awarded the international 'Defender for Democracy Award'. I decided not to share this information with my colleagues at Bal Ashram or Bachpan Bachao Andolan right away. Pradeep had expressed his desire to see Delhi and our home there several times in the past. I figured this was the best chance to get rid of Pradeep's deep-seated doubts about him being a bad omen. So when I left to receive the award, we took Pradeep with us to stay at our home in Delhi. The following day, I took him with me to the office. The organization's general secretary, Ramashankar Chaurasia, announced the award to our colleagues and gave the first piece of the traditional congratulatory sweet to Pradeep. He told everyone that we had received this award because of him. Pradeep's eyes popped out of his sockets in shock! He hid his face and began sobbing. It took a long time to console him. Everyone congratulated Pradeep for the award, delightedly exclaiming how lucky he had proven for the organization. He would look at me and then at Sumedha ji and me again. He was confused. There was disbelief in his eyes but he clearly felt joy. Later that day, we invited all our colleagues for dinner at home. Pradeep sang a Punjabi song, and danced all evening with several colleagues.

This incident left Pradeep deeply moved. But the self-doubt that he was programmed with since as long as he could remember would not be got rid of that easily.

'Bhai Sahab ji, is it true that I am not cursed?' he asked me. 'Did you really receive that award because of me?'

'Yes, this is true,' I replied. 'You are a good person, and no child can ever be cursed.'

Others confirmed what I told him and we could sense that he was beginning to let go of his fears.

In August 2001, Pradeep was enrolled in school. But the interest in studies that he had demonstrated earlier showed some decline initially. He had been enrolled in the second grade, and he passed with average marks. But in the third grade, he passed with a first division. Steadily, his personality began to blossom. He began participating in sports and cultural events organized by the school. In 2005, he participated in the Children's Congress organized in Delhi by Global March Against Child Labour and delivered powerful speeches against harmful traditions that hurt children. He had developed a keen understanding of the issues of child labour, child trafficking and education. Several of his interviews even appeared in newspapers and on television.

Many others among his peers in the Ashram used to participate, and still do, in child rights related events across the world. A number of them, including Kalu, Amarlal, Puran, Kinsu, Om Prakash and Shamsur, had never even been on a train before coming to the Ashram. They would call the airplane a *cheel gaadi* (eagle car). They would return from their trips with endless stories about their adventures and get a kick out of recounting them to the others.

Kinsu was a talented and bright child, and so had been on several such trips around the world. Pradeep was jealous of him, as boys his age often are, for this reason. Whenever it was time for Kinsu to leave, Pradeep would find the right moment and hide his luggage. Once he left, Pradeep would vent his bitterness by seeking out anyone who was looking to get a haircut and force one on them. Maybe this gave him some peace. It was possibly a sign of the presence of memories of home in his subconscious that he found peace in this activity. Our activists had informed us that though Pradeep's father worked somewhere as a driver, his maternal grandfather and uncle did indeed work as barbers.

Pradeep was entirely capable of participating in international events like Kinsu and the other children. The challenge was to get him a passport or visa in the absence of any valid identification. Sumedha ji had directed the manager of the Ashram to work on getting him a passport. Our capable manager, Adesh Kumar, prepared the request form, Pradeep's school certificate as proof of age, his Ashram enrolment documents, and signed on to be his legal guarantor. He approached the passport office with these, but his request was rejected. It was essential to have the authorized consent and signature of a legal guardian who was a blood relative. Despite all his efforts, Adesh could not succeed in getting Pradeep a passport. The unfortunate irony of the situation was that Pradeep was not an orphan; his parents did not accept him as their child.

I asked Adesh to make another attempt to contact his parents, to get in touch with his mother's relatives to help initiate a conversation. He personally visited Pradeep's village, but was met with the same if not worse welcome. Pradeep's family members hurled insults and verbal abuses at him. He returned, dejected. Back at the Ashram, he told Pradeep everything that happened and asked him if he would like to come with him to the village to see his family, as a final recourse. If even after seeing him the family did not accept him, we would consider the legal route. But Pradeep burst into tears as soon as his family was mentioned. He said he would prefer to kill himself before laying eyes upon his family again. He refused all food and drink, and insisted on speaking to Sumedha ji over the phone. He told her he did not consider anyone except her his mother. Sumedha ji assured him that he would not be sent to his parents without his consent. All of us decided that the matter be put off for now, even though it meant he would not be able to travel outside the country.

Pradeep was a fan of cricket. He was so obsessed with the game in fact that by the time he was done with the eighth grade he had abandoned his studies and could be found playing all day long. He would grab whoever was free and force them to play with him. My son, Bhuwan, was studying law at the time. He was very fond of playing cricket as well. Whenever he visited the Ashram, he would bring sporting equipment for the children. Especially cricket bats and balls since they would often break. As soon as he would arrive at the Ashram, having driven for five or six hours, Bhuwan would be accosted by the children and pulled away to play cricket. A cricket bat was handed to him before he had had a chance to have a drink of water. 'When will Bhaiya [elder brother] come?' was Pradeep's abiding inquiry, because Bhuwan would play with him for hours.

This cricket craze was obviously not unique to the Ashram's children. Cricket is the most popular form of entertainment in India. In 2010, Adam Gilchrist, the Australian cricketing legend, considered among the best wicketkeepers in the sport's history, was visiting India for a tournament. Through a friend in Australia, we organized for him to visit the Ashram. When this news reached them, the children simply lost their minds! Pradeep lost his interest in food or sleep. He would run to his teachers in the middle of the night to ask them, 'Is Gilly really coming to the Ashram? Are you sure we will meet him?'

Gilchrist had promised he would play cricket with the children at the Ashram, and he did just that. Thousands of young people and villagers climbed the walls of our Ashram to see the game. Many of them brought tractors and trucks to stand on top of to see the match. Pradeep was one of the children who got to bowl to Gilchrist. We had told him that he could do so only on the condition that he would go back to school. He happily agreed. He joined school again soon after and passed the ninth grade. But the following year, he failed his matriculation exams in Maths, English and Science. It was possibly the most emotionally and mentally tumultuous year for Pradeep.

That year, our activists had traced the parents of a child who had been staying at the Ashram for several years. His name was Vishal. He had gone missing at the age of four. He was rescued from Jaipur railway station. He had been taken by a criminal gang, and was used for begging and pickpocketing. He did not remember anything of his family or village. Listening to the language he spoke and the folk songs he used to sing, over the years we had tried to figure out where he could have originally come from. We shared our inference with the police, who approached a man from a village in the area we had narrowed the search down to. The man had registered a missing child's complaint several years ago. They showed him Vishal's photo. After due investigation, he was found to be Vishal's father. All of his family members walked three hundred kilometres to meet Vishal at the Ashram. Vishal too recognized them immediately. The entire Ashram, not just Vishal and his family, burst with joy. Between sobs, members of his family told us about their ordeal, how they searched every nook and corner for their missing child. Not only had they made the rounds of the police station, they had prayed at every possible place of worship. They published advertisements in newspapers. At the slightest suggestion that someone might have useful information, they would run to meet them. All without luck, of course. Vishal's parents said they believed they had been given a new lease of life.

Pradeep had never liked Vishal, but that day even his eyes were filled with tears of joy. When he was leaving, Pradeep couldn't stop crying as he hugged him goodbye. Later that night, we found Pradeep crying with his head buried in his pillow. He remained low the following day too. Bhadram, who had been staying at the Ashram for ten years, and Bhupati, who had been there for about six or seven, tried to console him. They confided in him that there was little hope their parents would ever be found, but that they were still happy. Since Pradeep knew where his parents were, they urged him to meet them, at least once. Maybe they would have a change of heart when they saw him. Pradeep remained silent, but their words seemed to have had some impact.

He was seventeen years old at the time. Our activists went to his village again. There they learnt that Pradeep's father had passed away. Following his death, the entire family had shifted to a slum settlement called Bansi, in Jaipur, which was his mother's place of birth. Coincidentally, a boy from our Ashram called Shamsul, who belonged to the same slum settlement, had returned home after completing his education and training. He was nineteen or twenty years old and was pursuing higher education while living there. Pradeep was friends with him. When we told him about Pradeep's mother and siblings staying in the same area, he eagerly began looking for them. Bansi used to be a small village adjacent to Jaipur city once. As the city developed, it turned into a slum settlement within the city. In the last two or three decades, India's second-tier cities have witnessed rapid growth and have swallowed many such small villages. This has compromised their rural character. Bansi, for example, was now populated with migrant labourers who had moved to the city from nearby villages in search of employment and other daily wage earners. Shamsul's family was one of them.

He and his brother searched for Pradeep's family around all the barbershops in the area, and finally found them. The family now consisted of his mother, elder sister and two younger brothers. Shamsul knew Pradeep's story. He cleverly explained to the family that Pradeep was now grown up and fully educated.

That he would start earning soon. The rest of the family was unmoved and cared little about Pradeep, but his maternal grandfather's heart melted. He asked Shamsul about any unfortunate events that might have taken place in the Ashram while Pradeep was there. Shamsul responded by telling him that, in fact, a lot of good had happened during Pradeep's stay there, and that he himself was an example of that. The man ultimately agreed to meet Pradeep.

The news reached Pradeep. All the children and staff at the Ashram convinced him to meet his family at least once. Although he dilly dallied initially, he eventually agreed. Ramkripal Guruji took him to Jaipur the next morning. Upon his return, he informed us that all of Pradeep's family members had accepted him and he willingly stayed back with them. I was away on a trip abroad at the time. It was Sumedha ji who called me up and informed me.

'I have some great news. Pradeep has returned to his family,' she said, overjoyed and emotional.

I asked her where he was, a bit impatiently. She told me he was in Jaipur, with his family. When I inquired if she had spoken to Pradeep directly, she said that she had. But she hadn't spoken to his mother, his elder sister or anyone else in the family for that matter.

After keeping the phone down, I tried to make sense of the situation. On the one hand, I was happy. One the other, I was sad at the prospect of being separated from this child who had stayed with us for nearly twelve years now. But then some doubts cropped up in my mind. The first question that bothered me was why the family did not wish to talk to the people who had taken care of their child for all these years. Secondly, what had caused this change of heart that led to the family accepting Pradeep after rejecting him twice? Maybe his grandfather felt sympathy for his grandson, but what about the other family members? I convinced myself at the time that the mother possibly felt regret for what had been done to her son. Or maybe, with the education of his sister, they had even overcome their superstitions.

A few days later, I returned to Delhi. I was still deeply anxious and uncomfortable about Pradeep. I first sat down with Sumedha ji and Ramkripal and listened to the entire story in greater detail. I heard the account of Pradeep's meeting with his family several times. They believed that both Pradeep and his family had embraced one another wholeheartedly. I dug deeper.

'For how long after meeting Pradeep did the family remain with him?'

Ramkripal thought long and hard and said, 'Not very long. His sister had to go somewhere, so she left within a little over half an hour. His mother has received a government job as a security guard, as a compensatory appointment for her husband's death. So she gave us some food, and left. His brothers seemed like vagabonds, and didn't stay home for long either. So yes, it was only his grandfather who stayed back and thanked Bal Ashram.'

'After meeting Pradeep,' I continued, 'did the family inquire about the past twelve years? Did they try to know more about his education, illnesses and the like during this time?'

Ramkripal took a moment to think and replied, 'No. No such thing happened.'

'Then we draw only one of two conclusions,' I told them confidently. 'First, that she is not Pradeep's mother. Second, they have not truly accepted Pradeep.'

That evening, I called Pradeep. I did not let my doubts and suspicions show. I only inquired about his general well-being.

'Bhai Sahab ji, *hai na*,' he said, 'everyone here is very nice. *Hai na*, they take very good care of me. They love me a lot. I am well taken care of, *hai na*.'

Having known him longer than his own family, I had observed that Pradeep would intersperse his speech with '*hai na*' (you see) whenever he wasn't sure of what he was saying, or was lying. I assumed that Pradeep was nervous on account of this major change in his life. I explained to him ways in which he can adapt to the new people, a new environment, emotions, experiences and challenges in his life. I encouraged him to complete his education and sit for his exams. He assured me that he would visit Bal Ashram in a few days to collect his books and other belongings. And that he would come back again for his exams for which he was enrolled in Viratnagar.

A few weeks passed before he suddenly arrived to meet his friends and teachers at the Ashram one day. He shared with them how he was welcomed and pampered by his family. Those living in the Ashram believed they saw a change in Pradeep's behaviour. He bragged about his new life back home. He acted as though he had won the lottery! Coincidentally, it was a few days before the festival of Raksha Bandhan (the Hindu festival to celebrate the bond between brothers and sisters, in which sisters tie a piece of thread around their brothers' wrist, who in turn promise to protect them). Sumedha ji gifted Pradeep new clothes for the occasion and gave him sweets to take back with him, to his sister in Jaipur. She was surprised that Pradeep didn't seem excited about bringing sweets for the sister whom he had spoken so highly of in the past few days. Still, she put him on a bus to Jaipur the next day.

I visited the Ashram soon after. He immediately came to meet me. I noticed the conflicted expression on his face, his forced smile right away. He was avoiding looking me in the eye. I didn't speak to him for long then, but called him after dinner. We stepped out of the Ashram for a walk. At first, we discussed his education, plans for the future and family, among other things. We then sat down. I placed my hand reassuringly on his shoulder before proceeding with what I had to say.

'Pradeep, listen to what I am saying carefully. I am not asking you for any answers. You don't need to react while I'm speaking.'

He nodded in agreement.

'Son,' I began, 'you've been trying to lie to everyone for the past few days. You used to lie to others earlier too, but not to me. This is why you're unable to lie to me today. You are scared. I know that your family has still not accepted you, and continues to hate you.'

Head lowered, he curled his toes to dig into the sand, while twisting and pulling at his hair with his hands.

I continued, 'You've been boasting to the people at the Ashram. You're scared that if they discover the truth, they'd lose respect for you. You're terrified you'll have nothing to fall back on. You think that if you tell the truth, you'll lose everything and will neither belong at home nor at the Ashram.'

Tears started to roll down his cheeks. I lifted his chin with one hand and wiped his tears away with the other.

'How many years of your life have you spent with your family?' I asked him.

He continued to cry. I placed my hand on his head affectionately and asked again.

'Bhai Sahab ji, five or six years,' he replied.

'And how many years with us?' I asked.

'Ten or eleven years.'

'So that means two times as close?'

'Yes, Bhai Sahab ji.'

I looked deep into his eyes. 'If we hadn't found them, would you have stopped considering the Ashram your home?'

'No, Bhai Sahab ji.'

'Then why do you feel this isn't your home any more?'

He said nothing and only wept. I embraced him and placed his head on my shoulder.

'If your mother accepts you, will you stop being a son to Bhabhiji and me? You'll always remain our son. Whether you stay with us or with your mother... Till the time you finish your education, find a job and are able to live on your own, you can stay at the Ashram just like you used to earlier. Whenever you feel like it, go meet your mother and siblings. Maybe they'll start feeling differently about you.'

Pradeep was now weeping uncontrollably, holding me like he would never let go. Consoling him, I made him stand up. I tried to say something funny to lighten the mood. We walked back to the Ashram together and entered the reception area. Nobody was there at that hour. I washed his face, made him drink some water and said to him, 'Now, tell me everything truthfully.'

He looked at me with his empty and desperate eyes and narrated all that had happened at home.

'Bhai Sahab ji, after Guruji left nobody except my grandfather even spoke to me properly. *Hai na*, Bhai Sahab ji. I had so much to tell my sister and brother. But they were not interested. The following day, when I went and sat next to them to speak to them, they got up and left saying they were busy, *hai na*. I told Guruji over the phone that, like Vishal, even my family loved me very much. I told Bhabhiji and you the same thing. I felt that the other children would respect me more if my parents were found. *Hai na*, Bhai Sahab ji. Everyone used to speak so fondly of their mother, father and siblings. They would even visit them during the holidays. So I lied, thinking about all of this.'

'You haven't committed any crime by lying,' I said. 'You lied because you were needlessly afraid. You have nothing to fear now. Tell your friends here the truth. By doing this, they'll respect you more, not less.'

'You are right, Bhai Sahab ji, *hai na*?' His eyes lit up as he said that.

'Come,' I said, 'let us begin by telling Ramkripal Guruji and a few boys and see how it goes. If you feel like they're making fun of you, or looking down on you then we'll end the subject right there. But if you feel their love and respect for you increase, then you will tell everyone the true story during the morning prayer tomorrow.'

Pradeep agreed. We called Ramkripal, Kinsu and Amarlal. It was very late at night, and they were obviously confused. Without any build-up, I told them that Pradeep wanted to tell them something but it should stay with them. Pradeep looked from me to them, and then hesitantly repeated the entire story exactly as it happened. They were shocked, but were overcome with emotion. All three hugged him. The following morning, he repeated the story in front of everyone. They were stunned. Like the night before, Amarlal and Kinsu came forward first to hug him. Following their example, everyone greeted Pradeep as though he was a long-lost brother.

Pradeep settled down after that morning. He began focusing on his studies. He was fond of cooking. In 2012, Sumedha ji heard of a youth skill development programme in certain fields which had been introduced by the Delhi government. A three-month course in culinary skills was part of the programme. A group of young students, including Pradeep, were enrolled for various courses. All of them completed the courses diligently. A few weeks later, when I visited the Ashram, I found a massive spread of delicacies laid out on the dining table. Pradeep and another boy, Shibbu, had prepared them. We appreciated their effort and rewarded them for it.

A couple of months later, Pradeep's uncle visited the Ashram with a friend of his. The middle-aged men showed a lot of affection for Pradeep. He took permission from his teachers and went on a trip to Agra with them. He was all praise for his uncle once he came back. He began making frequent visits to him in Jaipur, although he never spoke to us about his mother and siblings. Soon after, he told his teachers and the other boys there that he was interested in hairstyling now. His uncle made a good living from it and he wanted to do the same in Jaipur. He later began working at his uncle's salon.

An important factor behind Pradeep's decision to leave the Ashram to work for his uncle in Jaipur was the fact that his best friend, Deepak, had moved out too.

Deepak had left the Ashram after his marriage, with which he had set an admirable example for everyone else. We had rescued a few girls from a circus a few years ago. They belonged to the state of Assam. They had faced all forms of abuse and exploitation from the owners of the circus. One of the girls had faced such extreme trauma that she wanted to commit suicide. She believed that nobody would marry her. When Deepak heard of her pain and helplessness, he went to Sumedha ji and told her that he would marry her. He had always had a predilection for doing unusual and daring things which nobody else would ever wish to do. Little did we know that combined with compassion this trait would translate into something so inspiring. He went to the girl's village and married her in a simple ceremony. We were proud of both him and the courageous young woman he married. Deepak had learnt to drive and now took up a job as a truck driver in Assam.

A baby was born to them within the first year. He first shared the good news with Sumedha ji and me over the phone. They named their son Aditya. Deepak was often away from home, spending days at a time driving down the country's national highways. But whenever he returned home, he made sure to call Sumedha ji so she could listen to the baby boy's voice.

Once, five years after his son was born, he called Sumedha ji in the middle of the night. He was yelling and crying on the phone, delirious with anger. She tried to calm him down, but was quite shaken herself. She handed the phone to me.

'I cannot live any more,' Deepak cried to me. 'My wife and her family have snatched Aditya away from me. They've stolen all my belongings and left me. And now I have also lost my job. Now I will either kill myself, or them!'

We yelled at him in an effort to make him snap out of his delirium, and assured him that we would help him out. Somehow, we managed to convince him to come to the Ashram. He arrived a few days later. He became calmer after his short stay at the Ashram, and then left for Assam again to look for Aditya. Once there, he learnt that his wife had gone away someplace and that Aditya's maternal grandmother was trying to sell the little boy. He alerted some responsible residents of the village, who threatened the old lady and handed Aditya over to Deepak. He brought his son back to the Ashram, and both of them stayed with us for a couple of months. Then Deepak got a decent job with which to support himself.

Today, Aditya lives in the Ashram. He plays with the other children, a mischievous young boy. He is around seven years old now. Being the youngest, he is the most pampered of the lot. He is also very intelligent. He struggled to converse in Hindi early on, but is very talkative now. He reads well and is sharp in Mathematics. Whenever we go to the Ashram now, he has a long list of complaints of other children and demands for himself ready for his grandparents.

While in the Ashram, Pradeep had begun expressing his interest in girls and, like his best friend, was eager to get married. Perhaps this was another reason he left for Jaipur. He isn't married yet, though. After working with his uncle for a few years, Pradeep left that job. We heard he now works in a factory.

'Why Didn't You Come Sooner?'

This is the story of mountains, and the rocks that break away from them. Unseen and unknown tales were transcribed on these rocks over centuries. Some of them have been marked by eight-year-old Devli.

This is the story of our daughters and their remarkable determination, courage and struggle for change. It is the story of a spark that emerged from darkness and lit a million lamps. I live in the glow of these lamps. I welcome you to share in this light.

It was a bitterly cold January morning in 2012. We were gathered in Bal Ashram's courtyard for a forum to discuss how we could turn neighbouring villages into Bal Mitra Grams (child-friendly villages). There were around a hundred and fifty children, women, activists, chiefs as well as members of village councils. Soaking in the winter sun, we sat around listening to the inspiring stories of child leaders and activists, and participated with excited applauding and sloganeering for each other.

Suddenly, my eyes fell on Devli, who was sitting silently at the back of the crowd. I called her, asking her to come to where my wife and I were seated. The activists and all my colleagues from the organization knew Devli and of her relationship with us. She was my fourteen-year-old bubbly and beautiful daughter who had an endearing manner of exercising great authority and right over me and my family. So it was rather unusual for her to sink into one corner so quietly and not be with us.

After the programme concluded, I asked her, 'Is there something wrong today? Have your parents fixed your marriage?'

'No, Bhai Sahab ji,' she answered coyly. Then, covering her face with both her hands, she turned to Sumedha ji and hugged her tightly.

'*Bitiya rani*,' I said, playfully twisting her ear, 'something is definitely up. If not marriage, you've definitely been engaged. I'll not let go of your ear till you tell us the truth.'

Immediately, Devli turned into her normal self, and making a face, squealed, 'I'd have beaten him black and blue. Thankfully, I screamed my lungs out at him and he just ran away.'

I smiled. 'That's the Devli I know.'

But then I became serious. What she had just shared was not a matter to make light of. 'Did someone tease you?' I asked her.

'Who in the world has the courage to tease Kailash Satyarthi's daughter?' she said, laughing. There was pride tinged with naughtiness on her lovely face. Then she added, 'Definitely scared you, didn't I? I told that scoundrel to look at himself in the mirror once before trying to marry me. I told him that he ought to get his five-year-old sister married before coming to marry me. The stupid man ran away. He thought he could marry Devli!'

But I could sense anger mixed with playfulness in her breathless rant. Sumedha ji and I hugged and congratulated her for her courage. The others present there lauded her boldness too, giving her a loud round of applause. It was only later that she told us who this person was.

'There's a relative in our neighbourhood. He and his son have been after my father for several days. They're relentless. They say that I have grown old and should be married off. And even my father agrees.'

Devli was sent to the dormitory with the other female colleagues. But after some time, as I sat down with the children and my colleagues to have lunch, she snuck up behind me.

'Guess who?' she asked in a made-up voice, placing her hands on my eyes.

Without removing her hands, I answered, 'Seems like it's a little cat who's about to get married!'

Taking her hands off my eyes, she twisted my ears and said, 'I won't let go till you convince my father to stop my marriage.'

True to her word, she let go only after I made the promise, after which she joined us for lunch, snuggling between Sumedha ji and myself.

We first met Devli in 2004. A middle-aged woman had come to our Delhi office, accompanied by a man. She was a tribal labourer. The man accompanying her told us that he had been rescued from bonded labour by us many years ago. This woman, named Narayani, was his distant relative. She told us that she was employed in a stone quarry in Haryana (a northern state bordering Delhi), where several generations of numerous families had been working as bonded labourers.

'Please help us get out of that hell, sir,' Narayani pleaded with us. 'I somehow managed to escape with Kaka Sahib'—the man who was accompanying her—'but my ailing husband is still there.'

Upon further inquiry, we learned that all of them had been kept as slaves in a place called Charkhi Dadri in Bhiwani, Haryana. The traffickers engaged by the stone quarry owners had brought labourers from Jodhpur, Rajasthan many years ago. Kept there by force, effectively two or three successive generations of these people had been enslaved. All the men, women and children had to work endlessly from sunrise to sunset. Apart from verbal and physical abuse, sexual exploitation of the women and girls was commonplace in these quarries. The labourers weren't even paid their wages. They were kept under strict surveillance so that none of them could ever leave. Narayani had run away on the pretext of going to the toilet. She broke down and cried her heart out as she narrated her escape.

Such stone quarries are not only cut off from cities and towns, but also from law and order. Stone is an easily available natural resource and its plunder and black marketing is rampant in India. Most quarries are illegal and unregulated, and running them wouldn't be possible without political patronage and protection. Bribery and bloodshed are par for the course in bids to obtain government licenses for even those that are operated under a thin veneer of legality. Several such quarries are run as part of criminal empires.

We had been deceitfully summoned by quarry owners and beaten up in the past. But I didn't sense any deception in Narayani's story. I asked them both to stay back at the office. The following day, we dispatched two of our activists to conduct a preliminary investigation in Charkhi Dadri. One of them was Ramsharan, who had been associated with us for a very long time. He had been freed by us from a stone quarry in Faridabad in 1985. Both our activists roamed around the area for a week in the guise of agents who supplied labourers and returned after taking stock of the situation. They told us that the son of the chief minister had leased a small portion of the quarry anonymously. On the larger remaining part of it, mining was being carried out illegally. Our colleagues made it clear that we could not expect any assistance from the administration in this case.

A few days later, the general secretary of Bachpan Bachao Andolan, Ramashankar Chaurasia, along with five senior colleagues and me, reached Bhiwani. Before the day of the raid, we stayed in a small guest house around twenty kilometres from Charkhi Dadri. We left all our luggage as well as the cars with the Delhi number plate there. Even Narayani and her Kaka were asked to stay back at that guest house. We split up into two teams and left to survey the area where the raid was to be conducted. We had hired two taxis ostensibly for going to attend a wedding; we pasted stickers that said 'Ranveer weds Geeta' on the car to add veracity to our claims, and even dressed up for the occasion so no one would suspect us.

In the evening, our loyal and senior colleague, Rakesh Sengar, led an advance team and left for the quarry. Late into the night, they continued to hover around the quarry, while carefully staying at a distance of a few kilometres. I slowly moved closer to the quarry with Chaurasia ji and two of our associates. It was a rough road that led to it. We pretended that our car had broken down and stopped at a tea stall. We spent many hours sipping tea. Barring Chaurasia ji, all of us had had at least ten to twelve cups of tea. It was a bitterly cold night. We were aware that the gun-toting guard who kept watch over all the labourers went to his village to relieve himself and took around an hour or so to get back. This made five o'clock to six o'clock the best time for us to raid the premises.

We had hired a truck. As planned, one of our colleagues met us at the fixed time, i.e. 4 am, in the truck and we proceeded to the quarry with it. Narayani and her Kaka were also with us now. They were scared, and stepped out at the very end, after all of us in the cars had come out. Narayani kept an eye out for the guard even though one of our colleagues who was hiding in the bushes had seen him leave for his village. No sooner had we alighted that all hell broke loose. Some of the bonded labourers, panic-stricken, started running towards their hutments in a frenzy. Narayani yelled out to them, giving them instructions. When they saw her with us they calmed down and felt they could trust us.

'Hurry,' she said, 'collect your belongings and get into the truck.'

To speed up the process, we helped them onto the truck ourselves. We managed to rescue around forty children, women and men.

I seated a few of the children in my car, and drove away as fast as I could. The truck with the men and women followed me. The clothes of the children who sat with me in the car were tattered and torn. The wounds on their flesh could be seen through the holes in their clothes. Every such wound is a blot on human civilization. The frightened little girls were trying to hide their bellies and chests by hugging their knees. They simply could not make sense of all that had happened since morning. I made tentative attempts to talk to them. I tried explaining to them that they were now free from bonded labour and were being taken to a secure place. But they had never known freedom, or safety. How could they understand what I was trying to tell them? Maybe they assumed I was their new owner.

Just then, I remembered that there were some bananas lying in the back of the car. I asked the children on the back seat to distribute them among themselves. I thought they must be hungry, and might feel better after eating something. But no one picked up the bananas.

'Go on, child. Pick up that bunch of bananas and pass it on,' I gently repeated myself.

One of the children gave it to the child sitting in front. An emaciated girl and a little boy were seated next to me. I told them to pass on the fruit to everyone in the back and keep one each for themselves. The girl looked curiously at the bunch as she turned it around in her hands. Then she looked at the other children.

'I've never seen an onion like this one,' she said.

Her little companion also touched the fruit gingerly and innocently added, 'Yes, this is not even a potato.'

I was speechless to say the least. These children had never seen anything apart from onions and potatoes. They had definitely never chanced upon bananas before. Upon further cajoling, some of them started chewing on the bananas. But they were trying to eat the fruit without peeling it. Some tried to swallow it while others were trying to hide it in their palms after having spat it out. My imprudence had for a moment pushed me back a few thousand years. The difference between an unpeeled banana and a peeled one was the distance between slavery and freedom. I quickly tried to rectify my error and taught them how to peel a banana and consume it. Most of them tasted the sweetness of the fruit and probably relished it too.

They began sharing this new experience among themselves in their dialect. I was feeling their joy too. Just then, the little girl sitting next to me tapped me on the shoulder and almost screamed.

'Why didn't you come sooner?'

I instantly turned to face her. Her innocent, tear-filled eyes and pained voice laced with anger pierced my heart. I could tell that these words had risen from the depths of her heart, where they lay suffocating for years.

Her younger brother had passed away for lack of availability of medicine. Once, the quarry owners had beaten up her father and uncle and branded them with burning cigarettes. They had raised their voice against the sexual exploitation of the women and tried to escape. Even the tiny hands of the children, when wounded, were never tended. They couldn't even manage to get bits of cloth to tie around their wounds. This little girl had survived the entirety of hell in the eight years of her life. This was probably the first time that she could bring herself to trust someone enough to mouth the words, 'Why didn't you come sooner?'

That challenging question deepened the restlessness and anger that the issue of child slavery aroused in me. The child who posed this question was none other than Devli. She had put it to me, but it is one that needs to be answered by every person who speaks of faith, law, the Constitution, human rights, freedom, childhood, humanity, equality and justice. That question is as pertinent today as it was on that day all those years ago.

According to an estimate, there are around five million labourers employed in stone quarries in India. Hundreds of thousands among them are child labourers. Contractors and their agents pay tiny advances to impoverished families in backward areas and get them to come to the quarries on some false pretext or another. This is the organized crime of human trafficking that is often dressed up as migration or displacement. Usually, there is no record of workers in the quarries. In other words, children like Devli and her parents do not exist anywhere in legal terms.

To break up the stone, deep holes are drilled in it with powerful machines by skilled or semi-skilled workers which are then detonated with the use of gunpowder. The large rocks that are exposed after the explosion are broken down into smaller stones by adult men and women as well as children. The smaller children are engaged in removing the soil before the detonation takes place as well as removing the small stone chips after. Death is far from uncommon among these unskilled labourers who often get buried under the rocks thrown up by the explosions or when a quarry, unsteady from the shock, caves in.

These families are forced into situations where they must borrow endlessly from the contractors. Once trapped in the cycle of debt, it becomes extremely difficult to escape it because the owners charge arbitrary amounts of interest which the workers keep repaying. And this debt carries over for generations. Whenever the workers ask for their daily wage or express the desire to leave, they are reminded of the large debt that remains to be paid. Of course, if or when their meagre wages are paid, it does not mean they're no longer in servitude. Some contractors and their agents also run illegal outlets selling alcohol. The labourers are often provoked into either buying or borrowing drinks from these outlets. Once they get hooked to liquor, fights among workers and even domestic violence become commonplace. The quarry where Devli worked didn't have a liquor store. But her grandparents on both sides were trapped in debt and had effectively become bonded labourers. Her parents were born at the quarry. The contractors had got them married when the two of them had grown up. Devli and all the other children there, like her parents, were born as slaves.

We took everyone to Bal Ashram. It had taken us over five hours to cover the two hundred kilometres. It was nearly noon by the time we reached the Ashram. Our colleagues had spoken to the labourers during the journey, explaining to them that they were now free. They were also informed that they were quite far from their ancestral village in Jodhpur. It would take almost midnight to reach there, and locating the village would not be an easy task. And so, for a day or two, they would have to stay in Bal Ashram, which fortunately was on the way to Jodhpur. During that time, all the paperwork would also be taken care of. Though we had tried our best to explain all this to them, it was not easy for them to feel at ease. They all looked suspicious and fearful even in the Bal Ashram premises and started talking to each other in whispers.

Reassuringly, Devli and the other children did not feel the same way. As soon as they got out of the car, they cheerfully ran to meet their parents. Some children still had their bananas with them, holding them up for their parents as if it were an extraordinary object. The Ashram workers had already prepared food for all of them. We knew from experience that once people are assured of freedom and security, the one thing they all do is to eat heartily. Each child can consume more food than several adults combined. And that is what happened on this day too. The labourers were astounded by the behaviour of our Ashram colleagues. They had never been treated with such love and respect in their lives. The entire group was placed under the supervision of Ramkripal Guruji, who had for many years himself been a labourer in a stone quarry. He was at the time around forty-five years old and the Ashram's head teacher as well as assistant manager. He is an inspiration for all rescued children. We had rescued him from Faridabad in 1984.

Guruji took Devli and all the others to the Ashram's assembly hall where they were to stay for the night. As they entered the hall, one of the children who stayed in the Ashram switched on a light. Before we knew it, all the rescued adults and children started screaming. They began running helter-skelter, screeching, 'Run! There are ghosts here!' Even I was shocked in the beginning but then it occurred to me that none of them had probably ever seen an electric bulb before. Ramkripal Guruji assured them that there was nothing to be afraid of and took them inside the hall again. He switched the bulbs on and off several times. But they still didn't seem comfortable with the concept. Soon enough, however, turning the switch on and off became a game for the children.

After two days, they were taken to Jodhpur. By that time, they were all convinced that they could now live their lives the way they wished to. Our colleagues had spoken to the adults earlier about going back to their native villages and picking up new skills to earn a living. The children who wished to study or live at Bal Ashram would be relocated at a later date. Having met the other children from the Ashram, the parents felt confident that their children too would benefit from living there. Devli, along with her best friend, Manju, expressed a desire to stay back at the Ashram and study. Their families were happy to allow them to. After a few months, Devli, Manju and two more girls were called to the Balika Ashram (the centre for girls) in Delhi. She began focusing on her studies now. While she was obstinate and threw the occasional tantrum, Manju was shy and serious. Even though both of them were born in Haryana, they spoke their native Rajasthani dialect. They even sang and danced to Rajasthani songs.

Devli had learned to make small public speeches against child labour. While her own life experiences certainly propelled her into working for the cause, there was also a bit of a rivalry with Razia which motivated her.

Razia's story goes back to the time when our organization was leading a campaign against child labour in the sports goods manufacturing industry in India. There were thousands of children among the three to four lakh employed in the sports goods sector. Much of the work in this sector—including the manufacture of cricket bats and balls, badminton rackets as well as the sewing of footballs—was done in a decentralized manner in village households largely concentrated in the Jalandhar district in Punjab and Meerut district in Uttar Pradesh. The children were mostly made to sew footballs. We were trying our best to make consumers and sportspersons aware of the situation. We were also building pressure on manufacturers, importers and exporters while simultaneously being engaged in making the villages in these areas child friendly.

The population in these villages was predominantly Muslim. Literacy levels among them were abysmally low. Despite the fertile lands they occupied and the abundance of water, their income from irrigation was far from adequate. And so, most of them were engaged in the manufacturing of sports goods. In the year 2000, the tireless efforts of our activists led to several girls and boys leaving the work of sewing footballs and enrolling in schools. I have always felt inspired by them, especially the little girls. Their simplicity, energy and affection gives me the strength to continue my work. It is most heartening to see their hunger to move forward and their ability to lead others. It is no wonder that in most child-friendly villages, the elected Bal Panchayat (children's council) leaders are girls.

Once, at Mukti Ashram in Delhi, we had a meeting of these elected child leaders, who had not just stopped child labour and child marriage in their respective villages but also inspired the rescued children to join school. This assembly saw many female child leaders talk about their struggles as well as achievements. There was Razia from Nagla Kumbha, Zainab from Chandaura, Zeenat from Jaanikala, Fatima, Rukhsana, Puja and many others. They went on to create history by becoming the first female graduates or even post-graduates in their villages.

Up to that point, Devli did not have any such story to inspire the audiences. The stories narrated by the other girls were making her restless. Razia reported that, in collaboration with other Bal Panchayat children, she had successfully facilitated the enrolment of twenty-seven children in schools thereby preventing them from being employed as child labourers. The village school headmaster had colluded with the chief of the village council and together they were running a mid-day meal scam. They would dole out bad quality food in lesser quantities to save money, which they then siphoned off. What is more, they collected money from students on one pretext or another even though primary education was absolutely free of cost. The children had brought an end to all these fraudulent practices.

Almost the same age as Devli, Razia was a highly sensitive and emotional soul. At the same time, her grit and resolve were something to be reckoned with. Her accomplishments made news even in the neighbouring villages. The same fraudulent practice was going on in the schools there too. Along with the children from those villages, Razia and her companions devised a plan of action. They began with writing letters of complaints to the chiefs of the village councils. This effort bore no fruit. All the child leaders then carried an application to higher authorities who operated from the district headquarters. The senior officers promised to look into the matter as soon as possible. But the children did not stop there. They took the story to the largest daily. The publishing of this news caused a frenzy. Each headmaster not only had to tender an apology but also return all the money the students had been forced to pay. Everyone in Mukti Ashram lauded the endeavours of Razia and other child leaders. I hugged and congratulated her.

Devli was a little annoyed with Razia. After the programme was over, the children and the activists celebrated by singing and dancing together. Devli loved dancing. But today she sat in one corner, sulking. She would stare at Razia and Zainab every now and then. When, eventually, the other children pulled her forcibly to participate in the festivities, she challenged Razia.

'If you're so smart, come and dance with me.'

Razia did not know how to dance. And Devli was only looking for an opportunity to pick a fight with her. We managed somehow to pacify her that day. With time, as she took part in other events, Devli realized that she needed to focus on academics and expand her horizons. She understood that respect must be earned by service to others, like Razia and the other child leaders had done, not just to one's own self.

During her time at Balika Ashram, Devli would sometimes go to her village to see her parents. It was during one of her visits when officials from the land department along with some police personnel landed at her place. They demanded to see the IDs and some other land-related documents of her father among several other people. Born and raised in slavery, they had no such papers to show the officials. The latter threatened them with evictions. Devli immediately called the people at Bachpan Bachao Andolan in Delhi. They managed to stall the proceedings for some time. We had already filed several applications to the government requesting them to rehabilitate the families and help dig out the property records of their ancestors so that they could claim what was legally theirs. But no action had yet been taken. The officials would repeatedly intimidate them, which caused them a lot of anxiety. We fixed a date on which we would go to Jodhpur and sit on a demonstration in front of the district collector's office along with Devli, her family and others.

We occupied a spot in front of the main gate of the collectorate, which the district collector and other senior officials used to enter the building. It was a peaceful protest, but a little while later, a group of policemen came to disperse all those gathered there. The tussle continued for some time. We discovered that the collector had entered the office from the gate at the back. But we stood firm on our demand that the collector meet the families, address their problems and provide a solution and made it clear that we would not move unless that happened.

The police tried to surround and threaten us, but not one of us moved. We went on with our speeches and sloganeering and were even joined by some local activists and concerned citizens. After nearly four hours, the collector came out to speak to us. He took the applications the families wished to submit and ordered his officials to not try to evict them. He even assured us that all families would be rehabilitated under the tribal welfare scheme. Devli, who had been sloganeering with enthusiasm, was filled with joy at our victory. The day certainly left a deep impression on her.

'Unless we're united and stand for each other, we can't attain anything, especially justice,' she commented on the way back. Indeed, there was a discernible change in her attitude after this event.

Devli asserted her right most strongly over my son, Bhuwan. He had been nicknamed Sona as a child and Devli called him Sona Bhaiya. Bhuwan's entire childhood has been spent with these children. After completing his education in law, human rights and management, he began looking after the work of Bachpan Bachao Andolan. The children know and understand that Sona Bhaiya will stand by them in their struggles, whether on the streets or in the highest court of law in the country. It is no wonder, then, that Bhuwan is showered endlessly with love. But Devli's way of expressing her love for him was unique.

A funny incident that took place a few years ago can better explain what I mean. Bhuwan had bought a car on a bank loan. He had had a fascination for toy cars since childhood. After months of research, making comparisons between the various options available, he had finally decided upon the make and model of the car. He even chose the leather upholstery, upsized tyres and music system for his car with great passion and interest. One can imagine how dear this vehicle was to him.

Coincidentally, Devli was in Delhi at the time to participate in a children's leadership forum. She was filled with curiosity when she saw the brand spanking new car. Feeling entitled, she told the driver to open the car and let her sit inside. The driver told her and the other children to wait for some time before he could allow them inside. He said they could enter the car once Bhuwan came. But that wasn't going to stop Devli! In a fit of rage, she reached Bhuwan's office. He was in the middle of a meeting in his office in the basement, which Devli stormed into.

'Sona Bhaiya,' she said, 'how dare the driver say no to me sitting in your new car?'

Bhuwan diffused the situation by sending a colleague with Devli to ask to driver to let her sit in the car.

She jumped into it, triumphantly hopping from one seat to another. There was nothing the poor driver could do. He just went and sat on the steps outside the office. A little while later, satisfied and pleased, Devli stepped out of the car and went to the office, teasing the other children. But the story does not end here. Bhuwan was in for a shock that evening when he took the keys from the driver and unlocked his car. Devli had etched on all the seat covers as well as the roof of the car: 'This is Devli's brother's car. This is my Sona Bhaiya's car.' This was written in red and black permanent marker pens. But then, that's what you get with Devli as your sister!

It was obviously not possible to force this girl into a child marriage. Not that we were going to leave her side in this fight. The very next day after Devli asked me to intervene, we sent one of our most responsible colleagues to Jodhpur; Devli's family were daily wage earners on the outskirts of the city. He convinced her father, Hariram, and her mother not to get her married. I'm happy to report that she continued her studies and her involvement in social activism.

She became an inspiration for not just children but for numerous activists working for children's rights in India and around the world. In 2008, there was a convention on the right to education organized by the Global Campaign for Education, in Delhi. The Director-General of UNESCO, Mr Koïchiro Matsuura, and the Executive Director of UNICEF, Ms Carol Bellamy, were in attendance along with other dignitaries from the United Nations. Devli too was invited to the forum as a children's representative.

Once everyone left after the event, in which many different views on the importance of education were presented by the various speakers, she came up to me and whispered something in my ears. What she said really surprised me. Devli never could keep anything inside her.

'Can I speak the truth?' she said. 'I don't think these people work in tandem. They were just praising their own organizations in silos. Maybe they aren't accountable to anyone, that's the reason why millions of children still work as child labourers. And these officials just keep talking and giving speeches.'

I had to admit to her that there was some truth in what she was saying. These organizations no doubt did some wonderfully good work, which helped children across the globe, but there was definitely a need to do more.

In September 2009, Devli accompanied me to the United States of America. She had been invited to present her views on the right to education at the UN General Assembly in New York. The prime minister of the United Kingdom, Gordon Brown, and I, as the president of the Global Campaign for Education, were the organizers of the event which we called 'Class of 2015'. The aim of this programme was to inspire governments across the world to fulfil the promise of primary education for all by 2015, one of the stated objectives of the UN's Millennium Development Goals. With the annual convention of the UNO then taking place in New York, there was tight security around hotels and streets right up to the main UN building. The president of Afghanistan, Hamid Karzai, and some other heads of state were residing in the same hotel as us.

We were surrounded by sophisticated machines, spy cameras, armed horsemen, commandos and security personnel with advanced arms. We walked to the UN building on the day of the launch, passing through many security checks to enter it. Devli was curious, but she didn't feel intimated or scared at all. She finally told me what was on her mind.

'Aren't we better off than all of them, Bhai Sahab ji? At least we can roam around freely. Tell me, if these are world leaders, who do they need to fear?'

I tried explaining to her about terrorism and other dangers but I am not sure if she was totally convinced by my reply.

Accompanying the two of us from Delhi were Ablaawi, from the West African nation of Togo, who had been a domestic child labourer, and some associates from our organization. The event was attended by Gordon Brown, Australia's prime minister, Kevin Rudd, the queen of Jordan, Rania Al-Abdullah, Norway's prime minister, Jens Stoltenberg, president of Sierra Leone, Ernest Bai Koroma, a prince of the Kingdom of Saudi Arabia, the chiefs of UNESCO, UNICEF and ILO, the president of the World Bank, Robert Zoellick, the archbishop of York, John Sentamu, the rockstar Bono, Sir Bob Geldof and the heads of organizations such as Cisco and Intel, among other eminent individuals and heads of state. To my knowledge, never before had such a distinguished group of people gathered together to talk about children's education.

I was organizing the programme. An excited Devli, true to her spirited self, stepped onto the stage, smiling coyly. What she began her speech with put me and a colleague of mine who were translating in a bit of a spot.

'All of you are so fat and round. I've never seen so many round people in my life. I wonder what you all eat and drink. And how are all of you so fair? Ever since I've come to America, I'm surprised at the number of fair people I've come across.'

Anyway, she continued, 'I know all of you are very rich and very important people. You are presidents, prime ministers, queens and kings. I had never before seen such people in my life.'

The audience were exceedingly impressed by Devli's guilelessness and her honesty. They encouraged her with applause and laughter.

'Now, what can I say?' she went on, 'Hmm, I'll try... Okay... I'll tell you. I was a bonded labourer. I was born and raised in stone quarries. Since I was born till the age of eight, I only broke down stones. I had no idea what a school was. I had never seen a book, a pen or a pencil. It was only after I was freed that I realized what education meant. Now I know that education is the only thing that can illuminate lives. It can empower you and is the key to facing all challenges in life.'

Few were unmoved by the manner in which she narrated her life story. Everyone in the audience looked at her unblinkingly as she spoke her heart out, clapping every now and then at something she said.

She ended her speech by saying, 'I would like to add just one more thing. A poverty-stricken, tribal girl like me has vowed that I will not let a single child in my village stay uneducated. I will ensure that each one of them is enrolled in school. Today, all thirty-two children—girls and boys—go to school. They used to go to work earlier or just roam around aimlessly before. I collected funds from their parents and arranged for a teacher. Now there is a government teacher in the school. If a small girl like me can manage so much, then I'm sure all you dignitaries together can totally eradicate child labour from the world. Why can't you all make arrangements for the education of all children?'

The hall of the UN headquarters fell silent. It seemed like everything had ceased to exist in that moment. Then everyone in the audience stood up to give her a standing ovation. The British Prime Minister and the Queen of Jordan came forward and hugged Devli. Ablaawi and she inaugurated the campaign, 'Class of 2015', with their digital signatures on a computer screen. Their signatures were followed by those of several prominent dignitaries, after which numerous important declarations were made. Heads of governments, ministers and leading figures from various corporations promised grants for children the world over. The total amount of money announced in the grants was in excess of 450 million dollars. Never before had such an amount been collected for the children of impoverished nations. The sum was enough to provide basic education to almost fifteen million children across nations.

Once the programme was over, there was a long line of

people waiting to meet and greet Devli. She became a rather popular child activist for the right to education after this event.

We were immensely happy on our return from the UN building. We decided to celebrate by going to a fancy restaurant. The happy and thrilled Devli was humming a Rajasthani folk song. Our colleague, Owain James, Devli and I were vegetarians. So the three of us were served vegetarian food. But Devli did not even touch what had been given to her. She stubbornly insisted that she would only eat Indian food, like roti, daal, sabji or not eat anything at all.

'Of all the dignitaries who came to hug and greet me and shake my hands,' she said, 'does no one eat daal-sabji at all? Can't you all take me where those leaders dine?'

I tried explaining to her that the food before her was exceedingly delicious, but that didn't seem to matter to her. Upon requesting the employees of the restaurant, they took me inside the kitchen. I asked the chef to add some vegetables to rice and make something like pulao so that the child wouldn't have to go back to the hotel hungry. We managed the situation somehow. But the next day, we went to an Indian restaurant and devoured the rotis, sabjis and daal that they served. Devli had a fantastic experience this time.

We also took her to see some of the monuments and other landmarks in New York, like the Statue of Liberty, the Empire State Building, the Brooklyn Bridge, et cetera. The fact that a majority of the cab drivers we encountered were Indian or Pakistani really surprised her. At the Statue of Liberty, she chose candy floss over ice cream. Incidentally, the vendor churning out candy floss from the machine was a Sikh man from India. The ever-talkative Devli started a conversation with him. He was so pleased and happy that he didn't even charge us.

His associate was a Pakistani. As we strolled about the area, we noticed that this man had carried aloo parathas for the Indian. Both of them ate the meal together, from the same tiffin. It wasn't a strange sight for me to see Indians and Pakistanis together on foreign shores but Devli was intrigued. She believed that the citizens of these two warring nations must live like enemies wherever they were.

'Bhai Sahab ji,' she said, after I explained to her that that is not always the case, 'I now understand that there are only benefits if you are friends. Enmity costs a lot. Wars are so expensive.'

We returned to India the next day.

In 2013, Gordon Brown, who was now the Special Ambassador for Education in the UN, announced an award for girls who had done remarkable work in the field of education. He asked us to suggest a name for the award. I was in a bit of a dilemma because choosing just one girl from among Razia, Devli, Zainab, Rajkumari, Hemlata and others was a difficult task for me. Razia was in the twelfth grade at the time and wanted to pursue medicine. Since there was no one in or around her village who could help her prepare for the medical entrance exams, we had called her to Delhi and got her admitted to a coaching institute. She was staying with us for some months while preparing for the entrance. Devli too was in Delhi at the time for some work.

Our associates had suggested Devli's name for the award. I had myself narrowed down our list to a choice between Razia and Devli. After breakfast one day, I took Devli to one side and spoke to her about it.

'Should your name be sent for an award?' I asked her.

At the mention of an award, her face lit up. Then, after having thought about it for a moment, she said, 'Bhai Sahab ji, I have been abroad quite a few times and garnered a lot of respect. It would be nice if you send a new girl child's name this time.'

I probed further. 'Do you have any name in mind?'

She gave me three names, one of which was Razia's.

Razia was indeed deserving of the award. We too felt that it would greatly inspire other girls from the Muslim community if she was conferred the honour. So we submitted her name for it. By good fortune, she was even selected for it. It was a phenomenal piece of news not only for her neighbourhood but also for the media, social organizations and activists working in the field of children's education. Our Bal Panchayat celebrated this news with great pomp. Devli too gave a speech there and danced to her heart's content.

The efforts of Devli and the Bachpan Bachao Andolan had paid off with the appointment by the government of a teacher to the school in her locality. Later, a separate government school was opened there too. She used to call us on the phone quite often after she moved back to her village for good. The frequency of her calls has come down a bit. But then, she has little time on her hands with her two little ones taking up most of it. Yes, she got married a few years ago. She had chosen the groom herself. Unfortunately, we couldn't make it for her wedding, but we did speak to her partner. It was pretty clear from the conversation we had that she keeps him on a pretty tight leash! I tell her I'll pull her ears hard if her children ever complain about her. From the other end comes the familiar pleasing sound of her carefree laughter.

The Opening and Closing of Doors

This is the story of a house that has walls but no doors or windows. Those who live within are considered cultured, wealthy and educated. The house is spotlessly clean, yet it smells. It has shining objects in it, yet it is layered with soot. A well-stocked kitchen, yet hunger persists. Once upon a time, a little boy named Ashraf lived behind those walls. This story is about the breaking down of these walls, the debris that fell, and the strength of the human spirit which can open doors where there are none. It is also about the changing of mindsets, as well as the laws of a nation.

It was the year 2014. Sumedha ji and I had gone to attend our friend Arun Sharma ji's daughter's wedding in Ghaziabad. Sharma ji had invited more than a thousand people for this grand occasion. We were looking forward to meeting Ashraf there. He worked in Sharma ji's factory and stayed in their home in Ghaziabad. We hadn't met him for more than a year. We looked around for him but couldn't find him, so we decided to ask Sharma ji before we left. But just then, dressed immaculately in a suit, Ashraf came running towards us. He bent down to touch our feet, and we pulled him up and hugged him to give him our blessings as we always did. He had clearly been busy with the wedding arrangements. He had some special responsibilities to take care of so we could meet him only for a little while.

Ashraf looked happy that night. He had turned twenty-five just a few months ago.

'How are studies and work?' I asked him.

'Bhai Sahab ji,' he replied, 'my computer hardware work is coming along very well. Sharma ji has also given me a raise. I send almost the entire amount to my mother. I promise that I'll soon take my private exams too.'

I patted his shoulder and said, 'Glad to know you're happy with Sharma ji.'

His face shone brighter than before. Happily, he added, 'Some days ago, it was my birthday. I didn't even remember it. But when I reached home at night, I was over the moon to see Sharma ji's whole family waiting for me with a cake on the table.'

Meeting him gave us an immense sense of peace. On our

way back, Sumedha ji said, 'May Ashraf be protected from the evil eye. He was looking like a groom himself today. We should soon get him married.' We had promised his mother Phool Jahan that we would get Ashraf married in a grand ceremony after he finished his studies and was financially independent.

That was the last time we met Ashraf.

Ashraf's father was a tailor. But he had been unable to work for over fifteen years after being diagnosed with tuberculosis. He had passed on soon after. Phool Jahan used to sell eggs and vegetables to help run the household. She gave that up to take care of the small children at home once her sons started earning. Everything was going fine. We couldn't imagine in our wildest dreams that we would suddenly hear of Ashraf's death one day. Their neighbour had called us two days after the incident, telling us that Ashraf had had a high fever for almost three days. Even after being medicated, he could not be saved. He had come to visit his family at Sangam Vihar in Delhi.

Sumedha ji and I rushed to his place with some of our senior colleagues as soon as we found out. The twenty-minute journey to his Sangam Vihar residence felt like twenty years to us. It was way back in 1995 when we had carried a grievously wounded Ashraf to his home. The entire journey was spent praying and imploring the Almighty to save the little boy's life. Nineteen years later, moving through the same path, we were praying that his soul rest in peace, our minds filled with memories of him.

When we had first laid eyes on Ashraf, he was comatose, with a half-burnt body. We had a small office in Aravalli Apartments in south Delhi. The sole landline phone in the balcony rang one day and a local daily's reporter expressed his desire to speak to me. He was a resident of Sangam Vihar. I listened to him intently. What he had just relayed was alarming.

'Sir, I've just come to know that a child from our neighbourhood has suffered acute burns,' he told me. 'He is lying somewhere in Ramakrishnapuram Colony [RK Puram]. Maybe he's even dead by now. He was a domestic child labourer in a renowned government official's residence. I'm going to their home with the child's mother and some of our neighbours... If someone from Bachpan Bachao Andolan could come with us,' he continued, 'it would help our case.'

Apprehending the severity of the incident, I told the reporter that I would like to go there myself. Upon obtaining the address from him, Sumedha ji and I, along with the director of our organization, Narayan Singh, left for the place.

RK Puram was a residential area for senior government officials. By the time we reached the address given to us, the child's mother and neighbours were already there. The shocked mother was hugging the half-burnt body and screaming out his name, 'Ashraf! Ashraf!' but the little boy, his body writhing in pain, could hardly manage to even open his eyes. Narayan Singh ji and I carried the semi-conscious Ashraf in our arms. Both his hands, legs, shoulders, cheeks and face were fully burnt. His body temperature was very high. One look at the child's body and anyone could have guessed that he had been brutally tortured.

It was a Saturday. The main door of the house was locked. We knocked on the doors of a few neighbouring houses but the people inside would turn up the volume of their televisions and refuse to open their doors. This was a neighbourhood where supposedly educated and civilized people resided. The few residents who came out told us nothing about the people who lived in the house where the incident had taken place. But apparently they had forgot to remove their name plate. That is how we learned that the house belonged to a man named Hamid Hussein. He was not just a senior government official. He was the additional secretary of the Ministry of Agriculture.

We rushed to a nearby hospital. On seeing Ashraf's condition, the doctors refused to treat him. Precious time was being lost and we were forced to take him to a nursing home. The doctors there were of the opinion that he hadn't been in an accident, and that it appeared more likely that he had been branded with a burning hot metal object. Ashraf hadn't uttered a single word since we arrived at RK Puram. Though he had come to his senses after treatment, and was out of danger as the doctors informed us, he still couldn't speak because of the trauma and pain.

Our next stop was the RK Puram police station. The station house officer was not available when we reached. His subordinate said, 'Sir has gone out on his rounds. We don't know when he'll be back. We can't file a complaint in his absence. If you wish to wait for a couple of hours, you could. Or else, please come back tomorrow. When the child himself can't speak, and there's no witness to whatever happened, then who do we write the report against?'

With Ashraf's cries still ringing in my head and this uncooperative man refusing to file a complaint, I found myself struggling to maintain my composure. Phool Jahan was getting more restless and nervous with each passing moment. We had been unsuccessful in getting an FIR registered after having spent more than an hour at the station. Justice was a far cry with no one at the police station willing to allow even the first step towards it of lodging a report. Eventually, we picked up the prescribed medicines and took Ashraf and his mother to their home.

I spent the night tossing and turning in bed, overcome with anxiety, thinking of ways and means to get Ashraf the justice he deserved. The first challenge that needed to be met was to get Ashraf to speak about the incident. There could be no case without it since no witnesses had come forward. But he could do this only when he began healing from the trauma. He needed proper treatment so that he could regain his health. The next day was Sunday. Early in the morning, Sumedha ji, our ten-year-old daughter, Asmita, and a few senior associates from our organization reached Ashraf's house. It was a small hutment, on rent. In the absence of a proper sewage system, the drains overflowed with dirty water filling the neighbourhood with its stench.

We had asked Asmita to come with us so that Ashraf felt less intimidated. In her tender age of ten, she was already an extremely sensitive child and participated in our work with immense enthusiasm. She sat next to Ashraf's cot, her tearful eyes filled with anger, and started stroking his head gently. All of us tried to give strength to the child in our own way. We then called for some food and all of us had it with Ashraf's family. A few hours passed before we could see a ray of hope. Ashraf began telling his mother and Asmita about the incident with hand gestures. He then started muttering something after having a few sips of juice. What he said was truly unimaginable.

How he came to be employed at this house, Phool Jahan had already told us about. A neighbour of theirs worked as a house-guard in the RK Puram colony. He had informed her that Hamid Hussein needed a domestic worker and thus six-year-old Ashraf had been sent to the government official's house. The little boy was provided a little space to sleep in the verandah. His parents had never met Hamid Hussein. Ashraf was given the responsibility of getting up early in the morning to sweep and mop the entire house. He was also to take care of his master's three-year-old child. The mistress managed the cooking herself.

Ashraf now began telling us what happened on the day of the incident. Hamid Hussein and his wife were getting ready to leave for work. The wife was a school teacher. That morning,

Ashraf had struggled to get out of bed as he was down with a fever. Instead of giving him medicine, the couple took him to task for being lazy. They had their tea and breakfast, and said as they stepped out of the house, 'The boy's fever will come down if he starves the whole day.'

As usual, they locked Ashraf inside and left for their respective workplaces. The entire day, he writhed in pain and hunger. In the evening, the moment they stepped inside the house, they yelled at him again for the unwashed dishes in the sink.

Ashraf went on, 'After that, the owner of the house sat down to offer *namaaz*. The lady started boiling milk for their child. I used to feed the little one milk with my own hands. He was always very fussy and would throw a tantrum while having his milk.'

Ashraf broke down as he said this. Our only consolation was that he was able to talk and express himself a little.

'The little boy had almost consumed the whole glass of milk, only a few spoonfuls remained at the bottom of the glass,' he continued. 'I noticed that madam was cooking and sir was still busy with his *namaaz*, so I quickly gulped the remaining milk in the glass. I was really hungry. I don't know how they saw me have the single sip of milk. They dragged me to the kitchen. Sir was screaming that the boy is a thief. His hands need to be burnt. Then both of them held my hands. Madam heated a pair of tongs and they burnt my hands, legs and mouth. Look, they even burnt my stomach.'

Phool Jahan had been crying uncontrollably throughout. All of us sat around Ashraf seething with anger. We decided to take Ashraf to Justice Ranganath Mishra, who was the chairperson of the National Human Rights Commission (NHRC) and a former Chief Justice of India. We went to his New Delhi residence; it was a Sunday so the Commission office was shut. It was late in the afternoon. Thankfully, Justice Mishra was at home. The moment he was told that we had come, he called us inside.

Justice Mishra was utterly shocked when he saw Ashraf's condition. Whatever we had understood from what Ashraf had related to us, we shared with him. He reassured Phool Jahan and stroked Ashraf's head to comfort him. Then he proceeded to call someone over the phone. In some time, the director general of the Commission along with two senior officials reached Justice Mishra's home. Later, Justice V.S. Malimath, a former judge of the Supreme Court who was now a member at the Commission, also joined us. Justice Malimath is the epitome of compassion and humility. He is an inspiration to us all. To my knowledge, it was the first ever emergency meeting at the house of the Commission's chairperson on a Sunday. The deliberations went on for about half an hour. Justice Mishra ordered an immediate investigation into the incident. At the same time, he directed that Ashraf's treatment be started at the All India Institute of Medical Sciences (AIIMS), the most reputed government hospital in the country. An incident such as this could not escape media attention. Numerous leading Indian dailies published the news in detail. This was an eye-opening story of domestic child labour, now in the limelight for the first time in the country.

Domestic child labour is often a form of invisible slavery where, behind closed doors, children undergo unspeakable abuse and indignity while toiling for up to sixteen to seventeen hours a day. It is the contemporary manifestation of a feudal mindset, which allows educated professionals and influential people to enslave children from poor, helpless families for their comfort.

In India and several other countries, the tradition of hiring a house help has been prevalent for centuries. Not only is it prevalent, it is an acceptable norm in these countries. Until a few decades ago, women brought little girls with themselves as maids to their new homes as part of their dowry. After Ashraf's incident came to light, we publicly called attention to the fact that renowned government officials, ministers, parliamentarians, legislators and even judges engaged girls as child labourers in their homes.

We may also note that there have been cases of child labour and exploitation even in the homes of ambassadors and officers deputed to UN organizations living abroad. The maids in these homes aren't paid any wages; they are told that their salaries would be settled with their families in India. The employers even confiscate their passports so that the girls can't escape or go back to India.

Bachpan Bachao Andolan made arrangements for the best medical treatment for Ashraf and also for financial help to his family. He was recovering well and quickly. One night, Phool Jahan called me on the phone. The late-night call had me worried for a few moments. But the very next minute my eyes welled up and my heart lit up with pride.

'Bhai Sahab,' Phool Jahan said, 'some time back, Hamid Hussein had come to our house with a maulvi [Muslim cleric] and some other people. He apologized at first and then handed over a few bundles of notes to me saying that the money was for me. He even said that he'd get Ashraf's treatment done.

'Then he asked me to withdraw the case against him saying, "Whatever has happened has happened. Let's forget about it." I got so angry I screamed back at him... "Just take a look at what you've done to my child. And now you've come to buy off my son's agony and our pride with these notes?"

'Bhai Sahab ji,' she continued, 'that shameless creature then tried to convince me by reminding me that we belonged to the same faith. "That Kailash Satyarthi is a Hindu," he said. "How long will that man help you?" He said he was a devout Muslim and prayed five times a day. He would help us throughout our life. He took out another bundle of notes as he said those words.'

I asked her what her reply was.

'Bhai Sahab ji,' she said, 'I spat on his face when I heard him mouth such dirt. Then I took both the currency bundles and threw them at him. I told them, "Even if Allah came and told me to take the case back, I wouldn't listen to him. All of you deserve to die a miserable death. This is a mother's curse."'

Phool Jahan said that they left nervously but not before threatening her of dire consequences. The confidence and fearlessness in her voice made me proud. The self-respect and dignity she had demonstrated is what true piety consists of. Even as she battled abject poverty, sicknesses, helplessness and starvation, she did not bow down to those with prestige and power. She had shown that human dignity, self-respect and the ideals of justice are not just mere words taught in school or by religious preachers. To her, they meant something.

Individuals in such situations are not always able to withstand the pressure and intimidation. In 2005, Sumedha ji once received a call from a lady who informed her that a young girl was being kept captive and engaged as a domestic child labourer in a neighbouring house. The woman didn't identify herself, but told us that it was a house in the Batla House locality of Jamia Nagar. Sumedha ji and one of our associates, Sheetal Raina, reached Jamia Nagar. There they went to the address shared over the phone call, a first-floor apartment. When they stepped inside the house, they found it empty. But then a small girl of twelve or thirteen emerged from one corner of the balcony. She looked emaciated and terrified. There was a deep, pus-filled wound in the middle of her shaven head. Both her hands and legs along with her back were sore with wounds. Her name was Salma.

Sumedha ji and Sheetal managed to get her downstairs. They rushed her to AIIMS where the doctors declared that it wouldn't be easy to save Salma's life. As per the regulations, the police was called to take down Salma's statement. Some of our colleagues from the Bachpan Bachao Andolan had also reached AIIMS by then. Salma hadn't had anything to eat or drink for the last several days. Mumbling, she asked Sumedha ji for a biscuit. It was only after she took a few bites that was she able to speak a little. She was so utterly scared that she wasn't ready to let Sumedha ji leave. She held on to her hand as she lay there on the hospital bed. The doctors and the police, seeing her physical as well as psychological condition, allowed Sumedha ji to remain by her side. I too arrived at the hospital a while later. The doctors had by then taken her in for a brain surgery as the infection had spread to her insides.

From Salma's statement, we had come to know that she had been brought from Gaya district in Bihar to Delhi to work as a domestic maid 'servant'. The owner of the Jamia Nagar house was a doctor who lived in Dubai. Salma used to live with his wife there. She told us that the mistress of the house used to hit her repeatedly on the same spot on the head.

When I left the intensive care unit after a few hours and went down to the park below, I was stunned to see what was happening. A hundred-odd people had assembled there. Leading all of them was a local leader from Jamia Nagar and a few maulvis. The leader knew of me and recognized me. The crowd surrounded me on all sides and began to threaten me. Sectarian and fanatical thugs will often come out in support of such depraved people who enslave others. And political and religious leaders are always on the lookout for such incidents to expand their clout; I have never seen these leaders stand by exploited children. The crowd wanted to intimidate me, insisting that the owners were decent people and that we shouldn't register a case against them. They told me that if I agreed to detach myself from the case, their local mosque committee would bear all the expenses for Salma's treatment. Some people even said that as a Hindu, I shouldn't be meddling in an incident involving a Muslim girl.

I needed to think of something quickly. I took the political leader to one side and told him quietly that his intervention in this incident could cost him his career and that he could get ousted from his party. I showed him the name and number of a senior leader from his party on my phone and made to call him. The leader panicked at the thought of being chastised by his senior. I breathed a sigh of relief and told him that if he helped with getting Salma the justice she deserved, I would recommend his name to his party seniors. But he needed to disperse the crowd before all else. The leader understood and somehow managed to explain to the people that they needed to leave.

In the evening, Salma's mother suddenly made an appearance at the hospital. Salma's employers had flown her in from her hometown. We knew what was going on and tried to make the mother understand what her daughter had endured, but to no avail. In around three to four days' time, Salma's condition had started improving. We were now sure that her life could be saved. She was upset and annoyed with her mother, who was siding with the mistress rather than taking care of her. Salma's legal guardian was her mother, and so she was handed over to her. After she was discharged from the hospital, Salma's mother took her to the people who had shown up outside the hospital.

A few days later, we received a notice from a Delhi court. The employers and Salma's mother had charged us with kidnapping her, a minor. Thankfully, we had the doctors' as well as the police's statements when she had been admitted in the hospital to back our claims to the contrary. We also had the medical reports. The judge dismissed the case in the first hearing itself.

After almost a month, Salma came to meet us following an altercation with her mother. We were rather surprised but pleased to see her at the same time. She, on the other hand, was too embarrassed and sad to express the happiness she felt. We sat her down and gently explained to her that it wasn't her fault. We also made her promise that she would not go back to domestic labour even if her mother tried to push her back into it. A few years later, we were pleasantly surprised to see her as a new bride. She simply showed up at our office with her husband one day. We welcomed both of them with open arms. They promised us that they wouldn't allow child labour in their village or even neighbouring areas.

Towards the end of 1996, Ashraf was taken to Mukti Ashram for his rehabilitation and education. The Ashram, set up in Delhi in 1990, is a rehabilitation centre for rescued bonded labourers and child labourers, a place for education, training, empowerment and leadership building. We had come to know that Ashraf's ten-year-old brother, Shaukat, was working in a masala factory for Rs 150 a month. He told us that he wished to see his brother freed from the factory. We acted promptly and managed to rescue him too. The work of grinding various masalas, including red chillies, had started to weaken Shaukat's eyes. Not only was he suffering from skin diseases, there was also a burning sensation in his throat and stomach that never left him. We got him to Mukti Ashram and started his treatment. He lived in the Ashram for five years during which time we got him admitted in a neighbouring school. He was later admitted to a government school in Sangam Vihar so that he could live with his family. Shaukat was the eldest male child of the family.

One day, Justice Malimath called me to the NHRC office to speak about Ashraf. We talked at length about the various aspects of domestic labour. I shared with him my first-hand experience of working on the issue, and told him what I knew about the estimated figure of children in domestic labour, the hiring process and the harmful impact of labour on the children. There was also the economic aspect that needed attention. Justice Malimath understood the gravity of the situation. He requested us to provide a written record to the Commission so that legal measures could be taken to curb this evil which we immediately delivered to him. Along with the note we gave, we sent letters to members of both houses of parliament. We had also attached photocopies of Ashraf's story which had been published in the newspapers. We asked them to lawfully ban domestic child labour. A new campaign against the practice had thus been launched in the country.

Justice Malimath had succeeded in garnering consensus within the National Human Rights Commission regarding ban on domestic child labour. The Commission sent a proposal to the law ministry with a recommendation that domestic child labour be banned under the child labour law. The ministry claimed that there were technical complications involved and did not concur with the Commission's recommendations. This happened not once but twice. But Justice Malimath was not easily discouraged. He found a solution. The Commission recommended an amendment in the terms of service for all central government employees. The amendment meant to prevent central government employees from employing child labourers for domestic purposes. There was no need to change the existing child labour law for this. It was possible through a gazette notification. Domestic child labour by government officials was thus prohibited.

But the Commission did not stop at this. They sent a further recommendation for amendments in the terms of service of even state government employees. In about two to three years, almost a dozen states had agreed to this and accepted the recommendation.

This was a monumental success for us. We now had a powerful tool to force the hand of the government. We increased our efforts in this direction, asking everyone to implement the same principles that had been enforced on central and state government employees. In an effort towards greater awareness to turn this initiative into a mass movement, we were simultaneously working closely with members of parliament to garner support from them. Our raid and rescue missions were also highlighted in the media, which certainly brought more attention to the issue.

At last, in 2008, we at Bachpan Bachao Andolan, along with many other organizations working against child labour achieved a momentous and historical win. The Indian government finally made an amendment in the child labour law. Under the new law, no one could employ a child under the age of fourteen as a domestic labourer. Anyone flouting this law could be jailed for three months to a year and would be required to pay a fine of Rs 20,000. We had a grand celebration, joined by Ashraf and his family. This was, in fact, Phool Jahan and Ashraf's triumph. It was their perseverance, will power, bravery and honesty that had culminated in the victory.

Ashraf had always been a serious child. He would always think before he spoke of which he didn't do much to begin with. While at Mukti Ashram, he had shown interest in two things—art and singing. His paintings showcased the brightest colours. Maybe his art reflected his hope and positivity—a triumph over the anxieties and agonies of his past life. At the same time, his soulful singing brought to the fore the deep pain and anguish inside him. In the beginning, he preferred to be by himself. He never shared his food or other belongings with anyone else. The other children found him selfish and mean. Neither did he ever express any desire to meet his parents or call them to Mukti Ashram to see him. His elder brother Shaukat was the opposite.

Gradually, we saw the introverted and intelligent Ashraf beginning to show greater social awareness. He had come to understand the grave injustices that children born to ignorant and poor parents must face. He was certainly not unaffected by his father's illness or his mother's grief, but he also felt anger for having to share the family's meagre resources with so many siblings. There were six in his home—an elder sister, his brother, Shaukat, and three younger siblings besides himself. Ashraf felt deprived. Unable to share his feelings with anyone around him, he felt stifled and suffocated. So he avoided being with other children or in crowded spaces more generally.

One day, I called Shaukat and Ashraf to speak with them.

'Have your parents ever been to school?' I asked them, as our conversation turned to this subject.

'No,' they answered in unison.

'Have they ever had a chance to live in a place like this Ashram and learn about society and life?' I asked further. 'Like both of you have over the past few years.'

They again answered in the negative.

'That is the reason they can't think like you and continue adding children to the family,' I said. I promised them that I would speak to their parents personally.

Their eyes lit up at the prospect. Ashraf happily chimed in, 'Bhai Sahab ji, I'm sure our mother will listen to you and follow what you say.'

I called their parents a few days later. They complained to me like they had done before about Ashraf not visiting them at home. They felt he did not love them. I explained to them clearly why Ashraf behaved in such a manner. Giving them a myriad examples, I told them how troubles escalate with a growing brood of children. I also reminded them of the torture and brutalities Shaukat and Ashraf had had to undergo to be able to feed their siblings. After a few days, we got to know that Ashraf's parents had opted for a family planning procedure.

In the year 2000, Ashraf travelled to the United States of America to participate in our international campaign against child labour. The moment we came out of the Washington, DC airport, he turned around and shut his eyes. He was overcome by the sight of things the like of which he had never seen before. There were many young people there who were either bidding farewell to their loved ones or had come to pick them up—they were all clinging to each other, kissing each other. Ashraf didn't know where to look so he lowered his head and his eyes. We could clearly see the expressions of shame, contempt and shock on his face. Later, he encountered the same things in New York City. I understood his predicament, and spoke to him when I found the right opportunity. I told him about how cultures vary, how people have different mannerisms and ways of greeting in different countries. It was only after our talk that he looked a little comfortable. We had prepared him for many things before we left for the US, but it had never occurred to us to discuss this subject. This incident taught us that we needed to anticipate such scenarios and prepare the children before they travelled abroad.

In 2002, Ashraf was invited to Geneva for a week. There he participated in a programme organized by the International Labour Organization, among other conferences organized by various other institutions.

Ashraf completed his studies till the twelfth grade from a school in Buradi village while staying at Mukti Ashram. Given his interest in computers, we had planned to get him admitted to a computer training institute. But a mishap was waiting to happen. Shaukat had gone home for his holidays. There he contracted high fever which impacted his brain adversely. He had begun to lose his memory. Even as the fever receded after a couple of days it left his nervous system badly affected. We got a renowned doctor to treat him but he could never completely recover. Their father had been ill for quite some time. The mother's shop too had all but shut down, leaving her with no means of earning a livelihood. His sisters were growing up and some goons from the neighbourhood used to harass them.

All this made Ashraf terribly sad. He had turned eighteen. We realized that he needed to start earning to support his family, but felt that he should privately continue his education part-time, along with his job. Our friend Arun Sharma used to run a factory that involved working with computer hardware. The whole Sharma family was aggrieved when Sumedha ji narrated Ashraf's story to them. They immediately hired him in the factory, and he happily enrolled in a computer networking course alongside.

He was a dedicated worker and persevered in his studies. His younger sister had studied till the tenth standard and the younger brother had passed his ninth standard exams while Ashraf was still alive. Having saved some money, he even managed to buy a small plot near his hutment and build two rooms on that. He would start blushing if anyone broached the subject of marriage.

'Let Shaukat Bhaiya get married first,' he would say. 'And I must also ensure that my siblings are educated. Besides, I want to continue my studies so that, after earning a little, I can focus my efforts on eradicating child labour. I have made it a point to speak against the exploitation of children. Whenever I see someone exploiting children, I do not keep quiet.'

We called Ashraf to the Ashram one day after the new child labour laws and policies had been brought in and told him about them. The news made him very happy indeed. One particular thing he said stands out from the conversation I had with him that day.

'What is that one incident at Mukti Ashram that brings you the most happiness?' I asked him.

'It was when I first went to school,' he said. 'It felt as though all my sadness and pain would vanish now. I imagined myself flying high in the sky, and as I went, all the closed doors started opening one by one.'

His eyes shone bright and his voice was filled with passion as he said this.

Ashraf held in his palms the open sky, through which he soared courageously on the wings of his dreams. Every closed door before him was his to open. But fate had other plans. Still, history will remember that there was once a boy named Ashraf, the intense heat of whose scalded body melted millions of cages of enslaved children. His parting smile made possible the laughter of the children freed from domestic labour. Ashraf lives on.

'Can I Take Two Rasgullas for Abbu, Please?'

This story is of blades of soft grass trampled underfoot each day, of the tiny droplets of morning dew, of pristine springs bursting forth from the mountains, of untamed rivers and the flames rising in their cold waters. It is a story about angels, who come not from the heavens above but have taken birth in the harsh womb of the earth.

It is also about a centuries-old conspiracy, a twisted tale of the perverted male ego and how it veils the woman with lofty ideals of sacrifice, surrender and tolerance, while gnawing at her body, mind and soul. This is the story of a challenge to this conspiracy, and triumph over it.

It was the month of May in 2013. A woman named Parbhati from the Dolahar village in Lakhimpur district, Assam came to visit us. She was around forty-two years old. She told us that her elder sister's daughter had been kidnapped by a man three years ago. That she had come to Delhi in search of her thirteen-year-old niece. The girl's name was Nandi.

The districts of Lakhimpur, Kokrajhar, Naugao, Sonitpur and a few others in India's north-eastern state of Assam have become hotbeds for the trafficking of young girls. Once trafficked, the girls are either pushed into domestic labour, prostitution or even forced marriage. Thousands of local men and women acting as brokers are involved in this business of trafficking.

Parbhati went on to share with us that she and her sister, Rami, worked in the tea gardens to make ends meet. One day, Rami had run away from home. She passed away after a few years. But she had once made Parbhati swear by the Bible that she would take care of Nandi if anything happened to her. And despite several challenges, Parbhati had kept her word. She was thus overcome with worry when she came back from work one evening to find an empty house. Nandi was nowhere to be found, in the village or in the neighbouring areas. The very same day, a man named Stephen had also disappeared from the village. It had been months since, but Parbhati had not received a single tip as to Nandi's whereabouts. She did discover, however, that Stephen used to take girls to Delhi. Parbhati managed to collect a bit of money somehow and finally came to Delhi.

'I was totally bewildered when I got here,' she said. 'Delhi is like a sea of humans, and I didn't know anyone here. I kept moving from one place to another with Nandi's photograph in my hand. I even inquired about Stephen, but no one claimed to know anything. On the contrary, people were mocking me. I had no money left so I went back to the village empty-handed.'

Back in the village, she dug deeper and came to know for certain that Nandi had been kidnapped by Stephen. He would traffic girls for a placement agency named 'Babita Enterprises' in Delhi. The agency paid him Rs 6,000–10,000 (about 50–100 USD at the time) for each girl he supplied to them. The girls were sold as domestic labourers for anywhere between Rs 20,000–50,000 (about 200–600 USD). Someone had told Parbhati about us so she took the risk of coming to Delhi again.

We assured Parbhati that we would do everything in our power to look for Nandi. One of our senior colleagues, Manish Sharma, was tasked with looking for Stephen. In a few days' time, we had found out that Stephen was a broker for many placement agencies. But we hadn't been able to acquire his phone number or address. Our first stop was 'Babita Enterprises', where the owner, Praveen Kumar, outrightly denied knowing of anyone named Stephen or Nandi. We went on to register a case against Praveen Kumar and Stephen, but when Bachpan Bachao Andolan activists and police personnel reached Praveen's office, he had escaped. It was clear that they had been tipped off about the raid by people within the police department, without whose connivance human trafficking cannot take place. Our colleagues had to come back empty-handed.

On the same day, around 10 pm, we received a phone call at our office. The call was from a police station in Sonepat, Haryana. The policemen informed us that two of our colleagues from Bachpan Bachao Andolan had come to them demanding the release of a girl from her employer. They said that the girl's maternal uncle was also present with the activists and was asking that the girl be returned to him. The police wanted to verify this with us. We were rather shocked since none of our colleagues had even gone to Haryana. In any case, Manish Sharma and Parbhati went to the Sonepat police station the next day. They found out that Stephen and Praveen Kumar had brought someone along to pose as our activist. Stephen had called himself Nandi's maternal uncle. Nandi and her employer were both present at the police station. Stephen had whispered in Nandi's ear that if she agreed to call him her maternal uncle, he would send her back to Assam and also pay her some thousands of rupees as wages. Nandi had even agreed to this. What choice did she have?

Nandi relayed the whole story to Parbhati later. She explained how Stephen had brought her to Delhi, promising to get her a lucrative job here, and then sold her to Praveen upon arriving. A few days later, Praveen had in turn sold her to someone else in Sonepat for Rs 22,000.

Some police personnel were in collusion Nandi's employer and the traffickers. They threatened my colleagues and pushed them out of the station. After a full day's struggle, with them reaching out to the higher authorities, the officer in charge agreed to start the proceedings. Around 1.30 am, Nandi was produced before the magistrate. Eventually, she was handed over to Parbhati. Our team reached Mukti Ashram at around four with both of them. I met them a few hours later, at around eleven. Oddly enough, Nandi's face showed trepidation instead of the relief and happiness one would expect to see.

Due to the unavailability of rail tickets in the peak summer months, both aunt and niece had to stay at Mukti Ashram for a few days. During the wait, Nandi finally revealed perhaps the most complicated part of her story, one that caused her tremendous shame.

She was uneasy all the time. Even Parbhati became concerned about her behaviour at the Ashram. Nandi kept speaking of either running away or taking her life. Sumedha ji came to Mukti Ashram when we told her about this. She noticed that Nandi was not as excited about going back to Assam as everyone had imagined she would be. So she spent half a day with Nandi alone. Once again, Nandi expressed her desire to die as she believed that she couldn't face anyone any more. Sumedha ji understood what the matter was. With a little prodding, the sixteen-year-old girl shared that she was three months pregnant. As pained as we were by this information, we weren't surprised.

Nandi's employer used to physically abuse her. She was kept hungry, not allowed to speak to the neighbours nor permitted to step outside the house. She could only go up to the door to buy vegetables from the vendor named Sanjay. He was the only person she could speak to, that for a minute or two. He would talk to her affectionately. Nandi was an innocent girl, unprepared for the deviousness of the man she was dealing with. One day, when he knew she was alone at home, Sanjay entered the house through the roof and raped Nandi. She screamed and wailed but to no avail. There was no one to save her. Scared and helpless, Nandi narrated the whole story to the mistress of the house, who, instead of helping her, said, 'Keep your mouth shut or the consequences will be dire. This must be commonplace for girls like you. And another such incident or two will not make any difference.' Nandi could not escape because the house was locked. Nor did she have any money because she had not been paid a single penny for three years.

When we found out about this, our colleagues and lawyers visited Sonepat again. A case was registered against the vegetable vendor, Sanjay. This wasn't simply a matter of law and order, but also one of deep psychological damage to a minor girl, her rehabilitation into society and the future of her unborn child. It was of utmost importance to restore Nandi's will to live and her faith in society. After a few days of psychological counselling, Nandi and Parbhati decided to medically terminate the pregnancy. A relative of Parbhati worked as a nurse in Lakhimpur's Masihi Hospital, so she felt getting the abortion done there would be the best and safest solution. She left with Nandi soon after.

It had been only a few days since Nandi's departure when another alarming case from Assam was presented before us. It was the month of June. I was sitting in the meeting room of our office with some senior colleagues when a few people came to meet us. One of them was a young man from the Kokrajhar district in Assam. His name was Shamsul and he must have been about twenty years old. He was accompanied by a woman and some five or six men who were from Delhi. The woman named Sameena said she was Shamsul's aunt. She had a lot of make-up on. She was loquacious and sharp and must have been around thirty-five years old. She claimed that her niece had been kidnapped and was being held hostage in the Palwal district of Haryana. All the men accompanying her had come to rescue her and wanted our help.

These men had a politician-like aspect about them, and looked rather dubious. They were all well-built and were dressed in sparkling white trousers, clean shirts and white socks and shoes. They even had gold chains around their necks and wrists and carried expensive mobile phones. Sameena said that the men were her friends and had offered to help. Shamsul appeared an innocent lamb surrounded by wolves. Our suspicions thus raised, we asked the men to wait outside. Then we told Sameena to remain quiet and to let the boy speak. We noticed that Shamsul wasn't comfortable in front of Sameena and wasn't talking freely. He looked quite scared. Each time we asked him a question, he would nervously turn to look at his aunt before he said anything. Sameena seemed eager to answer all our questions and would invariably cut in with choice expletives for her niece's kidnappers. So we had to ask her to sit in one corner of the room. I then made Shamsul sit next to me to make him feel more comfortable. Patting his shoulder, I gently started talking to him. Shamsul kept his eyes lowered throughout as he told us about himself.

He was the eldest of three siblings. The youngest sister was Sahiba (name changed). They had lost their mother when Sahiba was just three months old. They grew up in an impoverished household, raised by their father, who was physically disabled.

All three siblings had started doing odd jobs at a tender age to make ends meet. Shamsul was speaking in rural dialects of Bengali and Assamese. He could understand Hindi but could not converse in it properly. With great difficulty, he told us about Sahiba.

'Once a boy with the same name as me, Shamsul, came to our village with his friend called Hovi. I have no idea how they befriended my sixteen-year-old sister. A woman named Haseena had helped the boys with it. One day, suddenly, all three of them disappeared along with my sister, Sahiba. She could not be found despite all our efforts. My father was deeply shocked by the incident. He would keep muttering Sahiba's name all day long and cry.'

Shamsul broke down as he narrated this to us.

'Last month,' he went on, 'I received a phone call from Sahiba from an unknown number. She whispered between sobs that she was in a village called Pingod, in Palwal district of Haryana. She was being held hostage at Barkat and Ikraam's home. She couldn't say anything more, but asked me get Rs 13,500 [about USD 150] to rescue her from there, or else she would die.'

When he went to the police station to register a missing person's report, the officer demanded Rs 40,000 (about USD 400). His father, Mujibur Rehman, had half an acre of land which could be sold for Rs 80,000. So the father and son sold the land and paid the police officer. He would go the police station every day but no action was ever taken. The money paid as bribe had been wasted. He only had a small amount of money left with him now. But Sahiba's phone call had raised his hopes and he came to Delhi. He somehow even managed to reach the village of Pingod and hunted down his sister.

'I just couldn't look at my sister,' he said woefully. 'She looked frail and worn down. Her face, hands and neck had injuries on them. There were wounds all over. It seemed like someone had bitten her. Her clothes were old and dirty. I started feeling dizzy and sat down on the floor. Soon, a group of men came and surrounded me. They were speaking in a language that I could not understand. There were two brothers. One was called Ikraam and the other's name was Barkat. Their mother and a sister were also present there. I offered Rs 13,500 at their feet and asked them to let my sister go.'

'What does she do there?' I asked Shamsul. 'Why didn't they release your sister after taking the money?'

'They started laughing raucously,' Shamsul said, 'and told me they wouldn't let Sahiba go for less than Rs 50,000. I begged and pleaded and told them that I had only Rs 1,500 more. They could take that too for my sister's release. Sahiba and I invoked Allah too but they threw me out of the house. I had to return empty-handed. I saw my sister lose consciousness as I was leaving.'

It took him almost half an hour to narrate the whole story.

He spoke haltingly. There was a language barrier between us. But it was also extremely difficult for him to share this with us. I would constantly wipe his tears and help him drink water.

'What work does your sister do there?' I asked him. 'Why have they not let her go?'

'Ikraam and Barkat have kept Sahiba in the house as their wife,' he muttered, pained and ashamed.

There has been for some time now a substantial disparity in the gender ratio in some states in India, with the males outnumbering females. This has contributed to the trafficking of girls from states with a higher female population to be sold in the states with a smaller female population. Haryana is one such state where the gender ratio is heavily skewed. We were taken aback by the complexity and seriousness of the case. After deliberating on the situation for a long time, we decided to put together a team of senior colleagues and lawyers and sent them all to Pingod with Shamsul and Sameena. The team reached Sadar police station in Panipat. They argued for hours with the officer, who claimed that the girl was an adult and that no proceedings could be undertaken by them. This despite the fact that Shamsul was carrying Sahiba's report card from her primary school which proved that she was seventeen years old. The station officer as well as his colleagues had never even heard of the laws that pertain to children in such situations, like the Protection of Children from Sexual Offences Act, 2012 or the Juvenile Justice (Care and Protection of Children) Act, 2000.

After several hours of persuasion, the police officers relented. A team was sent to the village with our activists. Pingod, a predominantly Muslim settlement, was around twelve kilometres from the police station. On reaching the village, the team was instantly surrounded by around two to three hundred people. They threatened them and let them know that the girl would not leave the village at any cost. Ikraam's family produced a marriage certificate too. They claimed that a maulvi had formally got them married with Sahiba's consent. (In India, the legal age for marriage of girls is eighteen years.) The certificate only made things harder for the police and our colleagues.

The policemen tried their best to explain the matter to the more reasonable among them, but it seemed like the mob could begin rioting any moment. My colleagues are experienced enough to handle such situations. Avoiding the angry crowd, they entered Ikraam's house from the back door, along with a lady police constable. With the mob out front baying for blood, they quietly took Sahiba out and left the place in one of the jeeps parked in the back lane. After the paperwork had been completed at the police station, Sahiba was sent to a women's rehabilitation centre in another city, Karnal, as per the directions of the local child welfare committee. That centre was around two hundred kilometres from Pingod.

The following day, Sameena confronted us. She claimed that Shamsul was a good-for-nothing young man and that Sahiba should be handed over to her. Shamsul did not have the courage to challenge Sameena to her face. But when we took him aside, he begged us with folded hands not to hand Sahiba over to her under any circumstances. Sahiba was still in the women's rehabilitation centre. Though Sameena, accompanied by her acquaintances, kept hovering around the centre to take Sahiba's custody, we managed to lawfully hand her over to Shamsul and move them to a secure location.

Sahiba was extremely frightened in the beginning but she gradually came to trust us a little and told us what she had gone through.

'My brother had bought me a mobile phone with his savings. Once, a boy named Shamsul called me and said that he knew me and that I was a really pretty girl. He said he would meet me when he came to the village. After a few days, he actually turned up in our village along with a friend. Shamsul would flatter me all the time. One day he professed his love to me and said that he wanted to marry me. He told me that he lived in Delhi. He said he knew my aunt, who in fact had given him my phone number. I fell for his bluff and without informing my father or brother, I ran away with Shamsul and Hovi and came to Delhi.'

Sahiba could speak better Hindi than her brother. We asked her if her family members would have objected to her wedding with Shamsul.

'We were very poor,' she lamented. 'My brother and father had mentioned that they would need to sell the land for my marriage. I thought I could save the land and at the same time live a decent life with Shamsul in Delhi.'

Sahiba was absolutely horrified to learn that they had in fact sold their land to rescue her. She tugged at her hair, her teeth clenched as tears began to stream down her face. She wept for what felt like an eternity.

'They would have died with grief if they hadn't found you, child,' I tried explaining to her. 'So what if the land is not there any more, at least they got you back!'

'It was hell!' she said after some time, when she had regained her composure. 'I have no idea how much Shamsul had charged his brother-in-law for me. The deal had been agreed upon at my aunt's place. She is not our own aunt. We call her that but she is not related to me. The man who had bought me, kept me locked up for some days. Then I was sold to Barkat for Rs 13,500. Barkat said that I had been bought for his brother Ikraam. On reaching his house, I realized that Ikraam was of unsound mind. Without getting us married, his sister shoved me into his room at night. I cried and begged before all of them, but they all treated me like an object.'

She was in a fragile state of mind. I told her that we would talk about this later. But it felt like she wanted to lighten herself by speaking out.

She was living in that house with her so-called in-laws and both brothers—Barkat and Ikraam—considered this minor their wife. She was of course a wife only in name. She was a domestic servant who was routinely exploited sexually. There was still some life left in her body but her soul had died an untimely death long ago. She walked around like a living corpse.

'I knew that my father and brother would do everything in their capacity to look for me,' she said. 'But I had lost all hope that I would ever see them again.'

Throughout this conversation, the doting brother, Shamsul, would at times smile at his sister or at other times break down in deep pain.

One day, I asked Sahiba what her favourite food was.

'Potato fries, rice and daal are what I love the most,' she answered.

We had already arranged for some rasgullas and other Bengali sweets. The siblings enjoyed the sweets. Then one of our colleagues appeared with her favourite meal. The little girl's face lit up when she saw the food. But suddenly, her smile vanished and she turned her face towards the ceiling, struggling to hide her tears. She didn't say anything to me but turned to Shamsul and said just one word, 'Abbu!' Shamsul assured her that their father was fine. Sahiba took a deep breath and sighed.

'God knows when he must have had his last meal,' she said. 'I was the one who used to prepare his meals.'

She kept stealing glances at the rasgullas. I assured her that all the sweets were for her and she could eat as many as she wanted.

'My stomach is already full,' she said nervously. 'But can I take two rasgullas for Abbu, please?'

I choked up as I said yes to her.

We informed both the brother and sister that criminal proceedings had begun against everyone involved in trafficking Sahiba, selling her and keeping her enslaved. Numerous cases had been registered under the child marriage, child sexual abuse and juvenile justice laws. They were both very happy when they heard this, and I imagine the rasgullas tasted all the better for it. The siblings were sent to their village discretely after a few days. We had packed a tin full of rasgullas for their Abbu. Back in her village, Sahiba began working towards making people aware about child marriage and child sexual abuse.

Proceedings were ongoing in the many cases Bachpan Bachao Andolan had lodged to get Nandi and Sahiba justice. Nandi had to come to Delhi again for a hearing. At the time, our daughter, Asmita, was pursuing a business management course in Hyderabad. So her room was vacant. We asked Nandi to stay there. Our sole aim was to prepare her psychologically for the case and help her remain calm during the process. She was very comfortable with us by then.

'Papa,' she asked me at the dining table one morning, 'how long will it take for my court proceedings to get over?'

Unlike all the other children, she had not called me Bhai Sahab. It made me deeply emotional but I did not let her see it.

'Why are you in such a hurry, child?' I inquired.

She looked down, and digging her toe nails into the floor, answered, 'My aunt has found a match for me. They want to get me married soon.'

I was elated when I heard this. I asked about the boy, patting her gently on her head. She said that all she knew was that the father of the boy had a concrete house. But she had heard from her brother-in-law that the boy consumed alcohol. Her face bore a look of sadness as she told me that.

'Papa, I am very scared of alcoholics.'

On probing further, she added, 'The man my mother had run away with was an alcoholic. He beat my mother to death.'

Speaking of her mother gave her a lump in the throat. Nandi was an adorable child, a cheerful and brave soul. I noticed that she was holding back her tears. She involuntarily picked up a fork and a knife from the table and began playing with them. Then she rolled up her sleeves to show me her injuries.

'Look, Papa, what that man did to me. He would beat up my mother without any provocation. When I tried to save her, he beat me up mercilessly too. He used to say that I should call him Papa. But how could I call that demon my Papa? One day he banged my head against the wall and I became unconscious. When I came to, I saw my mother's body slumped in one corner. There was blood flowing from her mouth. I tried waking her up but she didn't move at all. Someone told me later that she had passed away. She was buried after that. I was just five or six years old. Some days later, I was told that my father too had died. The place where I used to stay with my parents was around one and a half hours from the village. I pleaded with everyone to take me but no one allowed me to go. I could not even bid farewell to my father. Then one day I heard that my brother had passed away. I could not even go for his funeral.'

I was struggling to sip my tea. I could see the reflection of our broken world in her beautiful and innocent face. I couldn't understand how, when there can be no human existence without women, the progress of civilization has meant abandoning their right to dignity, independence and identity. This certainly did not happen spontaneously. It was the result of a systematic and calculated attempt by men to gain power and control. It seemed to me so utterly hypocritical how women are, on the one hand, made to feel helpless and weak, expected to compromise at each step of their lives, and on the other, upheld as symbols of fortitude, courage, bravery and sensitivity. How much longer are they to suffer this reality? The safety, respect and rights of our daughters ought to be the essential parameters to gauge the success of human civilization.

Just then, Nandi looked up at me with hope in her eyes. 'Papa, will you speak to the boy who's supposed to marry me?'

'Definitely,' I replied instantly. I became really emotional. 'Do your aunt, sister and the church priest like the boy?' I asked her. 'And can the boy make a promise in the church that he will quit consuming alcohol?'

'I don't know,' she replied. 'Please have a word with him yourself. His name is John.'

It was decided then that I would speak to John that evening. Then, fiddling with her hands, Nandi spoke haltingly.

'Papa, if I say something to you, will you get angry?'

'Even if I do get angry, will you not remain my daughter?' I said, patting her lovingly on her cheek. 'Okay, I won't get angry,' I added.

'The money that you had given me when I had been rescued is with my aunt. She had taken away all of it. I have just used Rs 13,000 to buy a mobile phone for myself...'

'But you aren't carrying the mobile with you,' I interrupted her. 'Where is it?'

'My cousin lost it,' she replied. 'I think he must have sold it off somewhere. And my aunt spent the rest of the money. But then I let it be. I thought, she's my aunt, after all. But now when I look back, I think she very cleverly took away all my money. I really don't know who to trust any more... And another thing, my cousin—my aunt's son...he behaves very indecently with me.'

I was listening attentively to all that she had to say. She was revealing to me everything in her life that troubled her.

'Can I tell you the truth, Papa?' she went on. 'When your colleagues had brought me to Mukti Ashram, I had felt very relieved and happy. But deep in my heart, I was also scared that maybe you will simply sell me elsewhere. I couldn't get myself to believe my aunt at all. I couldn't sleep when I was being taken from Delhi to Assam. I kept thinking about where your colleagues and my aunt were taking me. One activist from your organization even misbehaved with me on our way to Assam. When I saw my elder sister at home, only then did I believe that I was finally free.'

I was quite upset when I heard what she said about Parbhati and her son. The activist she had mentioned was of course thrown out of the organization soon after.

I had a long conversation with John that night. He said that he sometimes worked in the tea gardens and sometimes as a road construction worker. He claimed that he hadn't consumed alcohol after Christmas last year. I was utterly shocked when at first I heard John say he was fifteen years old. But he had a weak grasp of Hindi and I later realized that he probably meant to say twenty-five. I was not entirely satisfied, however, after my conversation with John. I told Nandi that she should not hurry into this relationship and wait for a couple of years instead. She would definitely get a better match than this. She returned to Assam a few days later, having readily agreed to my advice. Fortunately so, because I received a call from her some time later and she told me that John and Parbhati were conspiring to take away all the money that she expected to get after winning the case.

She had to travel to Delhi and Sonepat several times because of the pending cases. She would stay at Mukti Ashram and sometimes visit Bal Ashram with Sumedha ji. We had been on the lookout for a good life partner for Nandi. But she was soon smitten with someone herself. The boy reciprocated her feelings. Both of them were adults, so, respecting their choice, we gladly agreed to get them married. Nandi's wedding was a splendid affair, with three hundred guests apart from the inmates of the Ashram. Amidst a lot of singing, dancing and festivities, Nandi was married to the man she liked. After some months of court proceedings, she got Rs 2,50,000 as compensation, which she deposited in her bank account. A mother of two, Nandi now lives in Assam with her family.

‘Does One Need to Be the President of the United States of America?’

This story is about a dream, one that rides on the clouds in the sky, frolicking about on them. It is a tale of a poem of mine, with a rhythm and a meter, but one which sometimes decides to flow freely on its own. This story is also about priceless velvet rugs, woven by a heart filled with dreams and delicate but injured fingers.

This is the tale of a Musahar family's small courtyard where a neem tree flourishes, the leaves and the branches of which make way for the most beautiful golden rays of the morning sun. It is about a child who looked into the eyes of an American President and challenged him. This is Kalu's story. It is a story that gives me the feeling of having lost something deep within. Writing it has indeed been a difficult task for me.

Kalu is no more, our most promising companion, who left us when he was just twenty-three years old. As I write his story, I can almost feel his round, tanned and innocent face smiling up at me through the page. And with his broad and sparkling grin he is asking me: 'Bhai Sahab ji, what are you writing? Do you think your Kalu can die without ending child labour in this world?'

It is impossible to wipe off the impression Kalu left on the hearts of those who knew him. He had incomparable courage and resolve and was filled with love. One couldn't help but be affected by his charming candidness. Even the president of the United States of America, Bill Clinton, was taken by his honesty and forthrightness. The meeting between Clinton and Kalu was not just an interesting one, it was truly historic.

Kerry Kennedy, the daughter of the human rights crusader, Robert F. Kennedy, is a renowned human rights activist herself. She had authored a remarkable book in the year 2000, *Speak Truth to Power*, on the lives and times of fifty individuals from across the globe who had led struggles for human rights. There was also a chapter on me in that book. It was launched in September of that year by President Clinton himself.

All the people written about in the book had been invited for the release. When I received the invitation from Kerry, I was struck by the feeling that I couldn't legitimately claim sole responsibility for all the achievements I was being lauded for. So I wrote to her requesting that she invite a child to the event instead of me—a child who, after being rescued himself, had worked to free other children trapped in slavery. She replied saying that I should come myself and also bring a child with me. We began to discuss at the office likely candidates from Mukti Ashram, Bal Ashram or one of the villages where we worked who could accompany me. All the children and our colleagues zeroed in on Kalu. He was twelve years old then.

Kalu was born in 1988 to a Musahar family in the Madhepura district of Bihar. He had lost his mother when he was very young. He was the middle child in a family of three brothers. Musahars are considered to be the most impoverished and the 'lowest' caste in Bihar, associated by caste norms to the occupation of killing rats. The people of this community work mostly as either as agricultural labourers or rear cattle. Some migrate to other cities and take up odd jobs to make ends meet. Only fifteen to twenty per cent of the Musahar population in this area is literate.

A boy born in these social conditions and context was now at Washington, DC, the capital city of the United States of America. Many prominent and distinguished people were part of the book launch: the author, Kerry Kennedy; renowned photographer, Eddy Adams, credited with the photos in the book; famous playwright and director, Ariel Dorfman, who had dramatized our lives and work; and numerous Hollywood actors as well. Young Kalu stood out in this sea of people in his starched white pyjama, red kurta and jacket. Everyone present was curious to know who this child was. Several people came forward to meet and greet Kalu, shaking hands with him. I was acting as his translator. In a while, President Bill Clinton entered the auditorium. Ms Kennedy moved forward to receive him. Just then, the President saw Kalu. He came towards us, shook hands with the young boy, and had a word with him. The conversation was short, but it proved to be an immensely important one.

Kalu politely said to the President, 'I'm extremely fortunate that I was rescued from bonded labour and today I am able to stand before you. But there are more than 250 million children across the world who are still exploited as child labourers. They aren't as fortunate as me. Please tell me, what are you doing for them?'

President Clinton obviously hadn't expected the child to be so frank and outspoken. Maybe he believed that this was all stage-managed and we had prepared Kalu to ask this question because he took a sidelong glance at me. Even so, he spoke warmly about his government's efforts and anti-child labour policies, imagining that the answer would satisfy Kalu.

This was the second and final term for President Clinton. So he told Kalu that whoever succeeded him would continue the work of eradicating child labour from the world.

'Sir,' Kalu immediately retorted, 'does one really need to be the president of the United States of America to do something to end child labour? Even out of office, I am sure you can do something for children like us.'

President Clinton was visibly moved by his words. He patted Kalu on the back and embraced him.

A few days later, there was such incredible news that it made all organizations working towards ending child labour ecstatic. Before the end of his term, President Clinton increased the fund for elimination of child labour globally from $30 million to $150 million. There is no doubt that there must have been other strategic factors which contributed to this decision, but many of my American friends believed that the moral challenge posed by Kalu's emotional appeal played no small part in accomplishing this.

Kalu had been trafficked when he was five or six years old along with some other children from his village. He was someone who took great pride in articulating his thoughts well. He would narrate the incident of his trafficking too in a detailed manner.

'One day, four or five of us were playing outside the village. A trafficker approached us. He distributed candies among us. We had never had such sweets before and we really enjoyed them. Then the man said that he would take us to watch a movie and give us more sweets to eat. We had heard that the village elders went to the city to watch movies, and the movies had a whole lot of song and dance, amazing action and drama. We fell for what the man told us and followed him. It was like we were jumping into a dark well.'

The trafficker took all the children outside the village and put them in a bus which took them to the railway station. After they boarded the train, he fed the children more sweets. When they woke up, it was already morning. Their long night of slavery, however, had just begun. To Kalu, it felt like the night would never end.

'Our train halted at Allahabad [now Prayagraj] station,' he said, recalling the incident. 'All the children were taken to a village called Saraibheeti in a bus from there. Most of us had started screaming and crying by then. The trafficker took us to a place where there were already some twenty to twenty-five children who were making something. That trafficker handed us over to another person and received a big bunch of hundred-rupee notes. It was then that we understood that we had all been sold to the factory owner.'

Sometimes, he would ask rhetorically in his childlike manner, 'Tell me, are children commodities to be bought and sold? They sold us!'

His brain was sharp and imaginative. His heart was just as emotional. He penned myriad poems. Even his manner of speaking was poetic.

That factory was, in fact, just a house where carpets were woven. It was located in a small village in Allahabad district in Uttar Pradesh. This was the first time that the children had seen a carpet in their lives. The very day of their arrival, the children were made to sit in pits and taught how to weave them. The mechanism wasn't remotely a modern one. It consisted of two thick, round ten-foot poles stuck into the ground ten to twelve feet from each other. Two six-inch wooden planks, one on the top and one below, creating a rectangular frame between them, would be driven through these poles. This apparatus was called the 'kaath'. Then, extremely fine but strong cotton threads were wound around these planks such that the vertically drawn threads were stretched tight. The ground between the two poles dug up like a narrow drain, the children would dangle their feet in it to weave the carpet on these taut threads.

The regions of Mirzapur, Bhadohi, Allahabad and Varanasi in eastern Uttar Pradesh are home to thousands of such carpet-making units. Most of the carpets are exported to the US and Europe, thus making the carpet merchants very wealthy. They have links to politicians, law enforcement agencies and the administration. Most exporters run the entire show through contractors and do not own factories themselves. These contractors traffic children from poverty-stricken families in Bihar, Jharkhand and even Nepal.

Kalu worked in that place for around four years. He wasn't paid any wages or given any money in lieu of the labour. The children were made to work nearly sixteen hours every day, fed only watery daal (lentils) and poor-quality rice twice a day. They would be given a roti once in ten days. There was no holiday or playtime. Kalu's father didn't have the wherewithal to look for his son. He lived in a broken hut and could barely manage two square meals a day. Having still tried for a year or two, he had given up hope of ever seeing his son again.

We had recently rescued some children from a village called Ausanpur, which was near Saraibheeti. On the basis of information received from these children, we planned the raid and rescue operation in Saraibheeti. It was the month of May, or June, in 1997. A colleague was sent to the place to covertly reconnoitre the whole locality. He informed us that there was no clear path to reach the spot. The residents of the village could recognize any stranger entering the village from afar, and would naturally be suspicious of them. And since many of them were involved in the carpet-making business, they would assemble quickly and attack anyone they found suspicious. Such a thing had happened to me on several earlier occasions.

On the day of raid and rescue operation, the sun beat down upon us. The mercury must have touched 47 degrees Celsius. Saraibheeti village was located on a dirt track about five to six kilometres off the main road. We could reach the village only after having weathered hot and dusty winds and extreme heat. We trudged down the path, covering our faces with towels to beat the heat and the dry wind. We had chosen this time of the day because people stayed inside their homes in these scattered settlements on hot afternoons such as this.

Quietly, six of us entered the gallery of the factory unit. The owner of this unit was lying asleep in the hallway, to which his house was also attached. As soon as we entered the hallway, some of his family members appeared and blocked our path. They began screaming, shouting verbal abuses at us. The two policemen who had accompanied us disappeared from the scene, instead of helping us deal with the situation. Before we knew it, the owner had quietly slipped away too.

I kept moving with another colleague. In the middle of the long, tiled hallway, there was a small door which opened into a square compound. The brick wall in front of the compound had doors to three rooms with stone ceilings. The floor of the rooms was plastered with mud and cow dung. The bigger room had three sets of poles and the smaller ones had two sets each. Inside a room, we saw six children at the kaath, covered in sweat, their naked bodies wrapped in a thin, ragged towel, huddled in one corner. They were terrified and unable to stand. I comforted them and told them that we had come to free them, and that they would soon be reunited with their parents. Stealth and agility are critical during raid and rescue operations. Without losing a minute, we have to rush the children to the rescue vehicles, and thus have mere seconds to build trust with them.

Just then, we noticed the massive lock on the door to the large room in front of us. Our suspicions were raised. At that point, another woman accompanied by some neighbours came in and started shouting profanities and threatening us. It was a rather difficult task to get the woman to give us the keys to that lock, but we managed somehow. What we saw inside was shocking. Several children were hidden under bales of wool, suffocating. One of them was Kalu. Luckily, we escaped that place along with the children, whom we brought to our office in Mirzapur after completing the necessary legal procedures.

That night, Kalu and the other children narrated their heart-wrenching story to us. There were burn marks on Kalu's thumbs and fingers. We asked him about them. He spoke with immense strain as he explained the cause of those marks.

'We had to make knots and then cut the woollen threads. If we made even a slight error, the owners would slash our fingers with a sickle. And instead of first aid or any dressing on the wounds, they would fill them with the phosphorus of matchsticks. Then they would light up another matchstick and bring it near the phosphorus-filled wounds. All the blood, flesh and skin would burn and stick together.'

I had rescued children from carpet manufacturing units earlier as well. I was aware of the inhuman torture they were subjected to. But I had never heard of cauterizing wounds with a matchstick's phosphorus before. I have no the words to express the heart-breaking sight of Kalu lifting the clothes that covered his thighs, chest and back as he continued to explain what was done to him. There was no part of his body that wasn't marked with deep scars.

'This was caused by iron claws,' he said, pointing towards his chest. 'There are sharp teeth in the claws which cut deeply. Two of the wounds have healed but the scars of the deeper ones are still there. One day I was missing my mother and crying. If my mother had been alive, I wouldn't have been playing outside the village like stray boys, and the trafficker wouldn't have kidnapped me. I was extremely sad that day, so some of the threads got woven wrongly. The owner lost his temper and slapped me a few times. I told him that I did not to want to be there any more and wanted to go back to my village. He got very angry at this and hurt me with the iron claws.'

Kalu was a free spirit. He couldn't stop himself from speaking out against any injustice. Perhaps that was the reason for his body bearing the most number of scars. Those scars felt like a blight on human civilization. Like someone had used iron claws to scratch out the words compassion, humanity and mercy from the Geeta, the Quran, the Bible, the Guru Granth Sahib and every other sacred text. Or they had filled our very Constitution, our rule of law and our judicial system with incendiary phosphorous and set them ablaze.

After being freed, Kalu stayed in his village for some months. Thereafter, our colleague Ghuran Master brought him along with some other children to Delhi. All of them lived in Mukti Ashram for a few days. I too was there at the same time. Here, Kalu met other children who had been rescued from carpet factories. Among them were Nageshwar and Mohan, whose childhood had been similar to that of Kalu. Mohan was from Saharsa district in Bihar. He had been held captive as a bonded labourer for six years. That day, he narrated an astonishing story to all of us.

While he was in the carpet factory, Mohan often dreamt of his father. But he had stopped having these dreams after one tragic night. He had seen his father in a dream that night, after many days. He saw that his father was on a bed and was calling out Mohan's name, but Mohan was tied down by ropes. And then, his father breathed his last. Mohan had screamed out so loudly in his sleep that he woke up all the other children. Even as the other children pacified him and tried to quieten him, he kept calling out for his father between sobs that whole night. Mohan's father had passed away that very night.

Kalu became very emotional during this conversation. He started showing them his wounds. Nageshwar too now joined the conversation.

'Don't cry. Become a policeman with me and we'll take care of all the carpet factory owners one by one.'

'What will you gain by becoming a policeman?' Mohan asked. 'Policemen are in collusion with the carpet manufacturers themselves. I have seen it myself. Once, many policemen came to my village. A well-to-do landlord had got into a fight with his workers. The policemen feasted in the landlord's house and badly beat up all the workers. They didn't even spare the women, dragging them by their hair... I also saw one policeman visit the carpet factory owner regularly,' he carried on. 'He would take a lot of alcohol bottles and money from the owner. And also touch his feet.'

On hearing this brutal truth about the police, Nageshwar changed his mind about joining the force. He corrected his advice to Kalu. 'All right,' he said, 'then I will join the army. Then I shall see how Balla Patel escapes from me. Kalu Bhaiya, you also join the army.'

Kalu didn't hold it against Nageshwar, but there was never any feeling of revenge towards the owners in his own mind. Nor did he ever express any desire to join the police or armed forces.

Nageshwar was seven years old when he had been trafficked from his village in Darbhanga district in Bihar. He had been taken to a carpet factory in Bargai village in Benares (now Varanasi). The twenty-third of October in 1995 was Diwali, one of the most important Hindu festivals. It made no difference to Nageshwar and the other children in the carpet factory whether it was Eid or Diwali. But the rest of the village busy was preparing for the festivals of lights. The houses had been cleaned, whitewashed or painted to welcome the Goddess of Wealth, Lakshmi. The people were decked in new clothes, and sweets and savouries were being prepared all over. Households usually keep their doors open on Diwali, so that Goddess Lakshmi can enter without hindrance. Balla Patel, the factory owner, and his family were distracted by the celebrations. The doors to his house and the courtyard, like those of others, had been left open.

Nageshwar and his friend Ganesh took this opportunity to escape the factory before the Diwali diyas were lit. They knew that there was a river next to the village. They had been taken there a few times for their bath, under strict vigilance of course. The children believed that if they could somehow cross the river, they could escape this living hell forever. They managed to reach the riverbank. Both the children were adept at swimming as they were born in flood-prone areas. But they couldn't muster up the courage to brave the night's darkness and swim at that hour. As it was the night of Diwali, there were no boats available either.

Within minutes, Balla Patel and his brother had followed them to the riverbank. The children tried to flee as soon as they saw spotted them, but Ganesh was caught and beaten up mercilessly. Nageshwar saw his friend fall to the ground, and his stomach and chest being kicked repeatedly. Ganesh then spat out a glob of blood and lay still after that. The owners dragged his body to the river and threw him into it. Nageshwar ran back to the factory to save himself. When Balla Patel and his brother returned, he was weeping inconsolably. They tied him to a pole.

Outside, the village was aglow with the shimmering light of the diyas. Balla Patel and his brother exited the chamber and came back holding sparklers and firecrackers in their hands.

'I was surprised that the owner had brought firecrackers for me,' Nageshwar said, recalling the incident. 'I thought they took pity on me or probably didn't want me to speak about Ganesh to anyone. I had already decided that I would ask for forgiveness and promise the owner that I would never try to run away again.'

He choked up and his voice trembled as he continued.

'They lit up the sparklers and gunpowder-filled thick pencils. My hands and feet were tied and I wasn't wearing anything apart from my knickers. The owners started scorching me. I was screaming my lungs out.'

Nageshwar does not know what happened after that because he passed out. His screams were drowned amid the celebrations outside. The child was badly burnt, as were the ropes that tied him down. The ropes that held him captive were of course intact. His body lay lifeless on the floor and filled the other children who had witnessed this with fright. Still, they ran to him to douse the burning embers of the rope as soon as the owners left.

One of Balla Patel's neighbours had heard the child's screams and he became suspicious. Fortunately, the man was related to one of our colleagues in Benares, Shiv Prasad Chaubey. He called and informed Chaubey ji from an STD (subscriber trunk dialling; privately-run public telephone) booth. Mobile phones were not widely available in India back then. Our colleague reached Bargai village before dawn. With the help of the police, Nageshwar was rescued from the factory. He was taken to Benares immediately and admitted to a hospital. He was in such terrible condition that he could neither lay down, nor sit or stand. The doctors weren't sure if Nageshwar would survive the burns. When the police investigated the matter, Balla Patel and the villagers unanimously asserted that he had burnt himself while bursting firecrackers. The police accepted their claim. The doctors, however, insisted there were signs indicating that he had been deliberately burnt. But the relative who had informed Chaubey ji was not ready to speak to the police.

The most concerning thing, though, was that Nageshwar had lost his voice. He couldn't even mumble. He was in critical condition in the Benares hospital for over four days before our colleagues brought him to Delhi after consulting with the doctors. Lifting Nageshwar in my arms to take him out of the car felt like carrying the ashes of humanity, burnt down as retribution for seeking freedom. We wanted to provide him with the best care and treatment. It was unbearable to see him wince in pain every time someone so much as touched him. There was a liquid discharge from his wounds, which had begun to fester and stink.

After preliminary treatment at the hospital, Nageshwar was brought to the Mukti Ashram. The love and compassionate affection of the children and workers at the Ashram proved to be a far better cure than all the treatments we had tried for him. His wounds had begun to heal in a few months' time. He had started eating and drinking on his own too, and slowly begun walking. Soon, just like the other children, he had settled into a routine. However, despite all our efforts and those of doctors and psychologists, he hadn't spoken a single word. All the Ashram residents were happy that he had recovered, but at the same time, distressed because of his inability to speak.

One morning, I received a phone call from Ranveer, one of our colleagues at Mukti Ashram. He just said, 'Bhai Sahab,' and broke down. I was terrified, imagining that something untoward had occurred at the Ashram.

'Ranveer,' I said, trying to console him, 'you're like my younger brother. Has something happened in the Ashram or your family? Please tell me the truth. I will help you come what may.'

He collected himself before he spoke, 'No, Bhai Sahab, I was calling to share some really good news with you.'

What he told me moved Sumedha ji and me to tears. Nageshwar could speak. He had finally found his voice. We immediately left for Mukti Ashram.

Every morning, Nageshwar used to water the plants in the garden, which was to the left of the workshop. He was as usual busy with this task that day when another child happened to pass him by on his way to the workshop. He couldn't believe his eyes or his ears as he listened to Nageshwar humming a Hindi film song:

> *Gham ki andheri raat mein, dil ko na bekarar kar*
> *Subah zaroor aayegi, subah ka intezaar kar*
>
> (Do not despair in this dark night of sorrow
> Hold fast, the morning will surely come)

The child was overcome with happiness and began rejoicing in delight. Everyone rushed to the spot. Nageshwar had become silent by then and stood smiling in a corner. After much requesting by all the children as well as the Ashram workers, he hummed the song once more. This was all that was required for everyone to start celebrating. The singing and dancing went on for hours; sweets were distributed among all Ashram residents. Nageshwar gradually began to speak more. Everyone at the Ashram was excited about this rebirth of sorts. The story he narrated, however, filled them with indignation. But let's get back to Kalu's story now.

Kalu Kumar's first stay at Bal Ashram was from 1998 to 2000. Like the other children, he had been enrolled in a government school in the Sothana village nearby. He was an extremely conscientious student. One month after he began school, his teacher visited the Ashram to praise his hard work. He suggested that Kalu could be admitted directly into the second grade as he was a sharp and intelligent child. Kalu proved him right by completing his studies for the second grade in just a few months. Impressed by his performance, the school principal even helped him prepare for his grade three exams at the end of the term. We were hysterical with joy when he passed his grade three exams too with flying colours. He later even stood first in grade four.

There were plenty of reasons why Kalu had been chosen for Kerry Kennedy's book launch event. His personality shone with optimism. And it seemed like his smile was structurally a feature of his face. He was particular about cleanliness too. Every morning, he would take long baths and keep scrubbing his clothes to wash them. He even encouraged other children to maintain hygiene. Having lived together at the Ashram for several years, Kinsu Kumar's eyes still well up when he speaks of Kalu today.

'I never saw Kalu Bhaiya get angry when a child made a mistake,' he reminisces. 'He would find the right moment to sit with us and gently explain to us what we did wrong. If any of us fell even slightly ill, Kalu Bhaiya would abandon his own routine—food, water, play, studies—to take care of us. Sometimes he would wake up in the middle of the night to check on the children who were not doing well... When I first came to the Ashram, Kalu Bhaiya greeted me like he had known me for years. He would befriend all the new children who came to Bal Ashram. The way he would tell us about Bachpan Bachao Andolan and Bal Ashram, we all thought and believed that this was our second home, where we could dream big and also make our dreams come true.'

Vijay, another child rescued from bonded labour, spent a considerable amount of time with Kalu. 'With Kalu Bhaiya around,' he says, 'no one could ever be unhappy—be it the teachers or children. We were always surprised to see how Kalu Bhaiya knew who was grieving or lonely. He would crack a joke, and make the child feel light immediately. He would often have lunch or dinner from some other child's plate. He really loved us all. All of us would wait for him to have our food, because it would be accompanied by a valuable life lesson, but given in a light-hearted manner.'

Anything that Kalu chose to do, he would become completely immersed in it. He loved sports and played cricket, volleyball, badminton and table tennis while he was in the Bal Ashram. In cricket, he believed in playing long and hard shots rather than staying put on the pitch and playing a slow game. If he stuck around for a while, it would turn out to be quite an ordeal for the other team. His powerful batting would sometimes send the ball as far off the field as the meeting hall or the dining space. He would always be chosen captain of his team. The other children looked up to him for his spirit of sportsmanship. He even had the respect of the team they would be playing against. I often played volleyball and cricket with him. The competitiveness the children felt caused great excitement, making them feel agitated when they lost. Kalu, however, never seemed affected by it. And this fortitude was reflected off the field as well.

Apart from playing sports, he was also interested in writing. He really enjoyed expressing his thoughts on ways to end child labour and on the sayings of great men and women of the past and present.

On his return from the United States, he would share detailed and animated accounts of the trip with his friends. He considered the days spent there some of the most enjoyable of his life.

'Along with Bhai Sahab,' he would tell everyone at the Ashram, smiling impishly, 'I managed to enter the aeroplane but my heart was beating fast inside my chest. I kept wondering how this huge machine could fly. And if it stops mid-way, would we be left hanging in the air? I just prayed to God. Bhai Sahab tied my seat belt. I told him that I did not want to be tied. At least, if left open, I could have escaped. What if I remained tied and could not jump off at all?'

He continued, 'The flight had taken off and I suddenly had to urinate urgently. Bhai Sahab kept his hand on my shoulder for a long time and that dissipated my fear but my desire to visit the washroom became more compelling. Bhai Sahab had told me earlier that all amenities such as drinking water, food, toilets, et cetera, were available on the flight. But I had forgotten all of this because of my anxiety. After a long time, when I recalled that there was a toilet, I told Bhai Sahab of my problem. He took me to the washroom and explained to me how the door was operated. But I just could not muster up the courage to lock the door from inside so I kept it open the whole time. Bhai Sahab stood outside and asked me if I was doing fine. I drank more juice on the plane than I've ever had in my life.'

Kalu would narrate his memories from his stay at the hotel in Washington with equal enthusiasm.

'We were taken to a beautiful hotel. I am thankful to Ms Kennedy for putting us up in such a wonderful place. I had seen such a magnificent place for the first time in my life. We first entered a box-like room. Someone pressed a button on the wall, and just like that, we were on the tenth floor of the hotel. I told Bhai Sahab that this was like a flying machine. We had been inside for hardly any time, and we were transported to another place. He told me that this machine was called a lift. Even in India, tall buildings have lifts. Then I realized that people living in cities like Delhi and Patna too probably used such lifts to go up inside tall buildings. We then entered a big room which resembled a palace just as shown in Hindi movies. There were two large beds in the room. The mattresses were so thick that they were almost touching the floor. I was sure that these mattresses were meant for a king. But Bhai Sahab told me that one of the beds was for me and I should sit on it. I was a little anxious and did not know how to sit on it. I had never sat on a bed like that one, but Bhai Sahab insisted, and I went ahead and sat on it. If someone objected to it, Bhai Sahab would look into it, I thought. The moment I sat on it, I can't tell you how much fun I had. I jumped on the mattress non-stop and enjoyed myself so much...'

The narration of these experiences would be accompanied by such fine performances that the listeners could not help but laugh till their stomachs hurt. Kalu was a natural actor. He would play the role of Hanuman ji in the Ashram Ramleela, attaching a tail to his back and filling his mouth with air. He would even sing revolutionary songs with great flair and passion. In his early days at Bal Ashram, he had once stepped onto the stage and shared a joke. I still remember it.

'Once an elephant was bathing in a lake,' he said. 'A drunk mouse passed him by. He went up to the elephant and said, "Get out." The elephant did not bother with what the mouse said. Then the mouse screamed loudly, "Hey you, elephant, get out." The elephant came out angrily and asked the mouse, "Why did you call me out?" The mouse said, "Never mind. You can go back in. I was just checking if you had stolen my knickers!"'

He had narrated this while acting as both the mouse and the elephant. Kalu would often poke fun at himself and others in a light-hearted manner.

When he had spent almost three years at the Bal Ashram, Ghuran Master, who was one of the leaders of Bachpan Bachao Andolan, along with Kalu's father and elder brother, felt that he should be sent back to his village as his father had not been keeping well. His eyesight was getting weaker and he could not make enough money because of that. His elder brother had got married when he was a child. He was a daily wage earner and barely managed to eke out a living for his wife and children. We had also brought Kalu's younger brother to Bal Ashram so that he could get educated.

Kalu was admitted to a school close to his village. But he didn't give up his commitment to fighting child labour. He helped rescue dozens of children in and around his village and made sure they were sent to Bal Ashram for education. He also got many children enrolled in neighbouring schools as well. Whenever possible, he would visit Bal Ashram to participate in the programmes concerned with the movement.

Meanwhile, a terrible incident took place in 2004. The parents of some girls from Nepal had approached us to find their daughters who were enslaved in the 'Great Roman Circus'. The owner, his cronies and all the other workers there were known to exploit the girls. At the time, the circus was travelling to Karnailganj district in Uttar Pradesh. The circus owner was a mafia boss and had the backing of the local police, the magistrate as well as political leaders. When we reached the circus to rescue the girls, the owners and his goons attacked us violently. There were media persons present there at that time and the incident was broadcasted on some national news channels.

Kalu, still in his village, saw me along with Bhuwan and the parents of two girls in a grievously injured condition on television. He was deeply traumatized seeing my bleeding head, and went into a state of shock. The anger inside him suddenly found its way out. An otherwise calm and composed child, Kalu would walk around deranged, threatening to kill the circus owners. When the villagers tried to stop him, he would scream out loud and then start sobbing. He would start hitting himself violently with anything he could get hold of. Then he would suddenly become quiet and lay down for hours. He had almost stopped taking food and water as well. Though his family, along with his Bachpan Bachao Andolan colleagues, tried to help him with medication and care, it had little effect on him. I had to take a few days to recuperate and was only made aware of Kalu's condition much later. The moment I found out, I picked up the phone and called him. I tried to convince him that I was all right but he refused to believe me. He thought it was my ghost he was speaking to over the phone. For some reason, Kalu believed that I had died.

So we called him to Delhi and he stayed with us for a while. Along with his psychiatric counselling, all my family members and senior officials of the organization took care of him. It took many months for his condition to improve. He was taken back to Bal Ashram after that. He would visit his village once in a while. In 2008, he passed his high school exams from an open school in Rajasthan. Our organization would help his family out financially from time to time, but his father and brother felt that it was more important for him to earn a regular income instead of working for the movement, sloganeering and all the rest.

Given his capabilities and talent, Kalu was employed in the Bachpan Bachao Andolan as a youth activist. He was initially deputed to help out with the work of the Mukti Caravan (Campaign on Wheels) but he soon became its leader. He infused new energy into the campaign, achieving outstanding success in checking the lack of coordination as well as the growing indiscipline among team members. Some young activists had started consuming alcohol excessively, which led to a decline in the Caravan's credibility among the people of the villages it travelled to. He proved his leadership and management skills by reorganizing the campaign team and bringing about much-needed reforms.

The Mukti Caravan was a small bus equipped with campaign material, loudspeakers and other instruments. A group of young activists, who had been rescued as children by Bachpan Bachao Andolan, would ride to various places in it. They were trained in performing street plays and songs that raised awareness, and also wall-writing and oration. Even today, the Mukti Caravan goes around to protest against child labour, child marriage and abuse and to raise awareness about education in villages. When these enthusiastic and passionate young people get off the bus, playing their instruments and singing songs, they always pull a crowd, curious and eager to join in, be it a village or a busy crossroad of a town or city. These are songs of change, like this one:

Ghar ghar alakh jagayenge—hum badlenge zamaana
Nishchay humara durlabh atal hai,
Kaaya ke rag-rag mein nishtha ka bal hai
Jagriti shankh bajayenge—hum badlenge zamaana

(We will light up every house, we will change the world
Our resolve is unshakeable
Faith and strength run in our veins
We will awaken one and all, we will change the world)

Slogans such as '*Bharat padhega, Aage badhega*' (India will be educated, India will progress), '*Sabhi padhenge, Abhi padhenge*' (Education for all, education now), '*Yeh hi Rahim ke asli bande, Yeh hi sacche Ram lalla, Chalo inko azad karayein, Chalo desh ka karein bhala*' (These are the true children of Ram and Rahim, let us free them and serve our nation), '*Nanhe haathon mein auzar nahin, khilone do, kitabein do*' (Let tiny hands hold books and toys, not tools), '*Padhai ke liye azadi, Azadi ke liye padhai*' (Freedom for education, education for freedom'), left an indelible mark on children's minds and hearts in thousands of villages.

After some time, Vijay too joined the Mukti Caravan team. He once recalled an incident that happened in Uttar Pradesh. Kalu was talking to a crowd about sending child traffickers to prison. Suddenly, an angry man emerged from among those gathered and started yelling at him. He was a child trafficker. Watching him scream and shout, some other people joined him in doing the same. Kalu fearlessly carried on, telling everyone why child trafficking and child labour were evil practices. So the man came up to him and slapped him. Before the Mukti Caravan activists could leap into action, Kalu had turned his other cheek towards the man.

'Please slap me more,' he said, smiling. 'Maybe you'll feel a little less angry then.'

The man, ashamed, made his escape. All the people present there were astounded and became absolutely silent. Kalu continued with his speech. Many people in the crowd later cheered him and embraced him warmly.

Once a senior teacher in the organization slapped Kalu. He did not utter a word at the time, but went up to the teacher later and said, 'Guruji, I don't think your anger has ebbed. If you truly believe that it was my fault, please slap me a few more times.' The teacher did feel ashamed for his behaviour but he didn't apologize to Kalu. To date, he regrets his decision to let his pride get the better of him. Kalu may never have preached tenets like 'do no evil, say no evil, hear no evil', but these principles were his way of life.

His short life was full of astonishing occurrences. In 2010, he once took leave to visit home. While there, he left one day for a neighbouring village to meet a relative. He had gone out alone and did not return for longer than expected. It turned out that someone had kidnapped him on the way. Not to turn him into a bonded labourer or for a ransom—he had been kidnapped to be turned into a groom.

It is a common practice in some districts in the state of Bihar to spirit away eligible and young bachelors and get them married forcibly. Particularly if the young man is educated and earns well. He is forced to sit through all the wedding rituals and take home a bride. The kidnapping of engineers, doctors, government officials and other such professionals is planned years in advance. The groom's parents and relatives find out about the marriage long after it has taken place.

Educated and salaried young men from well-to-do families can easily cost up to twenty-five to thirty lakh rupees (USD 3,000–3,500) in dowry. Even grooms from impoverished families can cost up to Rs 50,000 (USD 500). Over and above the dowry, families must humour the whims of the groom's side, pay for their accommodation, the feasts and more. That is why the bride's side will sometimes resort to kidnapping the boy, getting him married to the girl and sending them away to start their new life. The groom's family is often left with little choice but to compromise. Mutual disputes between the families, however, can carry on for years.

Poor Kalu Kumar had to go through this as well. The whole neighbourhood recognized Kalu because of his famous picture with President Bill Clinton. How could the many fathers and brothers around him not have their eye on him? The person who was working to liberate others got caught himself! The girl's family had already set up the *mandap* (wedding altar). In a matter of a few hours, Kalu found himself dressed up in new clothes, wearing a wedding turban and entrusted with a new wife, Baingani Kumari. With no choice or say in the matter, Kalu returned to his village with his bride. His family and relatives didn't have a choice either but to accept Baingani.

Feeling utterly ashamed, he did not let me or any of his colleagues at Mukti Ashram know about this incident. But there were some noticeable changes in his behaviour and his companions now became suspicious. His smile had become wider and his meals more timely, and his clothes were as shiny as his face and teeth. Once, when he had taken leave to go back to his village, they called him at home. But Kalu was not there; he was at his in-laws' enjoying a feast of kheer and poori. He was really fond of good food.

He was hesitant to come to our place when he next visited Delhi after a few months. He knew that we were aware of his marital status. So I made it a point to confront him at Mukti Ashram. Kalu covered his face with his palms when he saw me. His shy smile still found its way through his fingers. With a bent head and lowered eyes, he started mumbling.

'What could I have done, Bhai Sahab? They forcibly got me married. I was alone and outnumbered.' Then, after a little while, he innocently added, 'I was very angry in the beginning, but when I saw your daughter-in-law, I thought, whatever happens, happens for the best.'

It must have taken the fast-talking Kalu at least two to three minutes to speak just these few sentences.

Whenever he came to Delhi and Bal Ashram in the coming months for work, he came without Baingani, and Sumedha ji and I would pull him up for it. Each time he would tell us, 'You'll have to come to my village.' What he hadn't mentioned to us was that Baingani was expecting. Then one day, we got to know that he had become a father. I garlanded him when he came to Delhi after the birth of his son. The colleagues and companions present there were surprised and curious about the reason for the celebration. As I congratulated Kalu, I told them all that he had made me a grandfather. They all stood up and clapped for the new father and came forward to embrace their favourite friend. He apologized to me and promised to bring his wife and child to the Ashram next time he visited. As far as my memory serves me, this was the only promise Kalu could not fulfil.

It was October 2011. The Mukti Caravan was campaigning in the mica mines of Koderma and Giridih in the state of Jharkhand. The Caravan bus had halted at a village in Koderma district. Street plays and public meetings would be held every day till late in the evening, led by Kalu Kumar. He himself acted as the narrator in our play against child labour, *Where Have the Children Gone?*. That night, he sang the final song of his life:

Inquilab ka naara lagate raho, saathiyon!
Bal mazdoori mitaate chalo, saathiyon!
Zaalimon ke zulm ko mita ke hum dikhayenge,
Shoshakon ke raaj ko hata ke hum dikhayenge,
Ek ho ke zulm ko mitaate chalo, saathiyon!

Hindu aur Musalman, Sikh aur Isaai,
Ek maa ke bete ho, mat karo ladai!
Saare bhed-bhaav ko mitaate chalo, saathiyon
Inquilab ka naara lagate chalo, saathiyon!

(Let's together raise the slogan of revolution!
Friends, let's eradicate child labour!
We shall erase the oppression of the oppressor,
We shall remove the rule of the exploiter,
Let us unite and end injustice, friends!
Hindu, Muslims, Sikhs and Christians,
We are all children of the same mother!
Let us remove all differences, friends!
Let's together raise the slogan of revolution!)

The whole village participated with enthusiasm. Everyone lauded Kalu and his friends' efforts. No one knew that this night of awakening was about to give way to a dark morning. The activists of Mukti Caravan slept in the corridor of a government school that night. Around 3 am, Kalu got up to relieve himself near a pond behind the school. A venomous snake bit him there. Kalu didn't see the snake so he assumed it was an insect that had bit him. He went back and lay down without disturbing anyone, as was his nature.

He lay there for several hours, with a cloth wrapped around the bite. When the pain became unbearable, he woke up a colleague and asked him for some chuna (quicklime). He had heard that it worked well as an antidote. His drowsy colleague handed over the chuna to him. But it seemed odd to him that Kalu hadn't asked for tobacco, or anything else that went with the chuna. The demand made no sense especially at that hour. He ran up to Kalu, and immediately suspected that a snake had bit him. Everyone scolded Kalu for not letting them know when the incident had occurred. He was rushed to a hospital where it was confirmed that it was indeed a snake bite.

It had been several hours now, and the poison had spread to the rest of his body. The hospital did not have an antidote for the venom. So his anxious and scared colleagues took Kalu to the district hospital. They had also informed our Delhi office. Kalu had lost consciousness by then. Though his condition had worsened initially, he seemed to be getting better with the treatment at the district hospital. He came to his senses the next day but the venom had impacted his brain. His speech was garbled. He threw away the medical drip and refused to let himself be injected with anything. Our family and everyone in the organization in Delhi were kept updated about his health. When his condition began to deteriorate yet again the next day, the doctors advised that he be taken to a private hospital in Dhanbad. His condition began to improve there. Senior members of Bachpan Bachao Andolan, Dhananjay Tingal and Mukhtar-ul-Haq, were by Kalu's side throughout his treatment.

Once Kalu regained consciousness, I would call him at regular intervals and request him to have his medicines as prescribed by the doctors. He used to listen to me. We were very hopeful that Kalu would recover soon. But just a few days later there were signs of rapid deterioration in his kidney. Given how serious his case was, Kalu was transported from Dhanbad to Durgapur in a state-of-the-art ambulance and admitted in a top super speciality hospital there. The doctors were successful in neutralizing the snake's venom. Kalu was responding well to the treatment he got here and it seemed he was finally out of danger. We were convinced that he had won the fight against death.

I had to go to the US for a few days to attend an event at that time. The programme was related to launching a campaign against agricultural child labour. Kalu's cheerful face was the only thing I could think of the entire time. Even though we were now sure that he would recover, my heart and mind were still in turmoil. I remember it was at my friend Rohit Sharan's place, where I was staying in Washington, that I got to know that Kalu's health had started deteriorating again. He was undergoing dialysis for blood transfusions twice a day. I tried to get a chance to talk to him on phone all day on 17 October, but he had been unconscious since morning. My phone rang around midnight in Washington. It was already 18 October in India. I picked up the phone fearing something untoward. It was a text message from Bhuwan with just three words: 'Kalu has left'. This news was among the saddest in my entire life. I was shocked beyond words. The little angel had left us.

As soon I returned to India, I left for Kalu's village with Ghuran Master and Mukhtar ji. We made our way through unpaved winding paths full of dust and mud to his house in the Musahar colony. It was a small dwelling with some of the tiles on the roof broken. Half of it was a room made of mud, with a small courtyard in the front. This was the only family property he had from his birth till his death. There were some plants in the courtyard that had been planted by Kalu. Sobbing behind her veil, Baingani put her son Satyam on my lap. Kalu had named his son Satyam. When I picked up the little boy, tears of both joy as well as grief rolled down my face. I had no strength to speak even a single word.

All the women, men and children of the hamlet were crammed into that small courtyard and the narrow lane that led to it. I almost felt like Kalu was looking at me through all the faces present, smiling and teasing me.

'Bhai Sahab, didn't I say you'll have to visit my village? See, I have won!'

With Satyam at my chest, I would turn from the flowers

planted by Kalu to the rays of the setting sun, peeking through the clouds. I could see Kalu in everything. Through Satyam's chest, I could hear Kalu's heartbeat. The very heartbeat I had heard when I had pulled him to me in the dark room of the carpet factory all those years ago.

We were there for several hours. There was a prayer service held for Kalu with the whole village in attendance. Our friends talked about many of the important events in his life with the gathering. We had known that he had received a job offer in Mumbai. But when Ghuran Master told us the full story, we felt even more love and respect for Kalu and that much more miserable for his passing. In 2009, Bachpan Bachao Andolan had launched a public awareness campaign in Delhi, in collaboration with a large media company. Kalu Kumar had spearheaded the campaign with his Caravan and the media company officials were thoroughly impressed with him. They reached out to our office and expressed an interest in hiring Kalu for their creative team. They offered to provide Kalu accommodation in Mumbai and, in his first year of training, a stipend of up to Rs 25,000 which could be doubled in the subsequent year. It was a matter of great pride and joy for all of us in the organization. He was asked to reach Delhi immediately so that he could leave for Mumbai and take up the job as soon as possible.

The offer came at a time when he was the sole earner in his household. His father was in urgent need of a cataract surgery and the house needed repairs too, for which there was no money available. Along with her in-laws in their broken hutment, his wife would await his return from his Mukti Caravan trips which often kept him away from home. It was all but decided that Kalu would go to Mumbai and start a new and happy life there.

During the prayer meeting, Ghuran Master recounted his conversation with Kalu in detail. Kalu had visited his home one day.

'Everyone is advising me to join the media company,' he said to Ghuran Master. 'I know that the advice is sound. But when I have been freed from slavery once in my life, why should I work for someone again? They are businessmen. They will sell my story and become richer themselves... Maybe they are hiring me for my capabilities. I am truly grateful to them for that. But they should know where this ability comes from. Didn't it come from the movement? How can I, then, leave the very movement that has made me so capable? That too, for some extra amount of money? I cannot do this. Master ji, please tell me one thing—have child slavery and child labour been eradicated yet? Are all the children enrolled in schools? If not, then how can I leave Bachpan Bachao Andolan? I will not give up this fight till I die.'

Baingani followed our advice and married Kalu's younger brother, Turanti. They live in the village. The hostel where Kalu lived in Bal Ashram has been renamed Kalu Kumar Hostel. Some time ago, I lost to Kalu's son, Satyam, in a race held in front of that hostel. He has been living in the Ashram for almost a year now, and is being educated there. Satyam's wide grin after defeating me made feel like Kalu will always win.

Even as I write this, I feel like Kalu will suddenly burst into my room without knocking on the door, as he always did. Flashing his innocent, sparkling white smile, he will touch my feet and say, 'Bhai Sahab ji, look! Your Kalu has come!'

The Leap of Dreams

This is the story of a sapling, which sprouted from the seed of fear. It grew to be a plant, whose own seed carries dreams within it. It is about that plant which carefully protects those dreams. This story is one of struggle, like that of a honeybee, which painstakingly collects the sweet nectar of life. You will find in this story paths paved with compassion, resilience, fortitude and enterprise. It is a story of helping others on their journey and about one's own self-discovery.

Omaanku, the child who once feared the cacophony of the wild, now has a voice that is heard far and wide. This is his story.

It was July 2019. Omaanku often visited the Bal Ashram but he had come for an important matter that day. One look at him and I knew he was in deep trouble, so I walked him to the side and sat down with him. He finally came to the point after beating about the bush for some time.

'I wanted to introduce you to a girl. If you'd like, I could call her here right now.'

I wasn't surprised at all. I said, 'You live in Jaipur, how will you call the girl right now?'

'She could reach in the next two and a half hours or so,' he replied.

I twisted his ear. 'Oh! So that means everything has already been decided and you just want me to give you my blessings.'

Feeling shy, he bowed his head. 'No, Bhai Sahab ji, both of us are really good friends, but have never spoken about marriage.'

'All right,' I said, 'tell me the story of your friendship first. We can talk about marriage after that.'

'The girl's name is Mona,' Omaanku said. 'Maybe you remember her from the Bharat Yatra. She had participated in the Yatra two years ago.'

The name did sound familiar but I couldn't recall her face. So I asked him to tell me a little more about her.

'Mona has completed her education in BCom from the same university as me. We taught slum children together, as part of the school project. She is currently employed with a company,' he added.

'Did you two get to know each other while studying together

in the university?' I asked him. 'Or did you know each other before that?'

Omaanku smiled. 'The story of our friendship goes way back. I'll tell you about that some other time. Actually, Mona is from my district itself. I have known her since she was in the tenth grade.'

'So do both of you really want to get married to each other?' I asked him bluntly. 'If yes, then what is the problem?'

'I really love Mona and she feels the same way,' Omaanku replied, 'but neither of our family members know anything about our friendship...'

'So you suspect that your family members will not agree to this relationship?' I interrupted him.

'Yes, we are Gurjars and her family is Brahmin,' he added quickly. 'No one in our locality has had an inter-caste relationship like this. So I don't think our families will agree at all.'

I told him I would prefer to speak to Mona before anything else. Omaanku dialled her number and handed me the phone immediately. After speaking to her, I was convinced that the girl was truly in love with Omaanku. She was very socially aware, and I also felt that she had more courage and greater clarity than Omaanku on the question of their marriage. I assured her that they had our blessings and promised our cooperation in this. But I also told her that it would still be better if they could try and convince their parents.

After a year and half of that conversation, on 23 January 2021, Omaanku and Mona rescued twenty-six bonded child labourers with the help of the magistrate and the police in Bhiwadi, Rajasthan.

'It was a porcelain factory,' Omaanku told me excitedly. 'The moment we stepped in, there was such a strong smell of gas that it was difficult to stand there. Mona and I were wearing masks.

But the policemen who were with us were unable to stay inside and came out. We realized that the children would have been suffocating inside.'

I told him to tell me about the incident in greater detail.

'I had learnt from the Bachpan Bachao Andolan office in Delhi,' he continued, 'that there were some bonded child labourers in Bhiwadi. I went there on 14 January. Further investigation took me to the place where the children were housed and I found around eight to ten of them sleeping on a terrace. Their entire bodies were covered in white powder; I couldn't even see their faces. I had been informed that the children had worked through the night, so I did not wake them up. With a rescue mission planned in detail, we reached the venue again on 23 January. However, we didn't find any children there that day. When we looked deeper inside the same compound, we found other factory units that were being run in the two adjacent buildings. There we found six girls and twenty boys working. They had all been trafficked from Bihar, Uttar Pradesh, Madhya Pradesh and other states. The youngest child was just eight years old.'

I lauded Omaanku's zeal and asked him about the policemen's behaviour during the raid and rescue mission. He informed me that the police team had been of great help in the rescue.

Although he had been involved with rescue missions earlier as well, this was the first time he had worked with his friend Mona, and they managed an extremely successful mission. That was in fact one of the main reasons for his happiness and excitement.

'Come on,' I said, 'don't delay it any more. Go ahead and get married.'

'Our parents will not support us, that much is clear. So we have decided to go ahead with a court marriage,' he replied, and then added, somewhat hesitantly, 'We had wanted to get our marriage registered on your birthday in January... But I was a little scared to ask you.'

Omaanku's real name is Om Prakash. I think I'm the only one who calls him Omaanku. I shall narrate the story of how he got this name later. Om Prakash had been rescued from agricultural child labour in 1999. He was around nine years old at the time. He is currently an activist with the Bachpan Bachao Andolan. He may choose to move on eventually, but I am sure that this hard working and ambitious young man will keep working to improve children's lives wherever he is.

'Sometimes it rained when I worked in the fields or went out to graze the buffaloes, cows or goats of the villagers,' he once told me, remembering the time before he came to the Bal Ashram. 'And sometimes, there were jackals and foxes too. I would tremble with fear...and often simply because I was drenched in the rain. And when I couldn't find any shelter, I would break down crying. I'm still scared of the sounds of the jungle... I remember my first day in Bal Ashram really well. When the other children and I were handed new clothes, I thought we were all getting married. Wearing new clothes was like a dream for me. I had never even thought that I would be allowed play time or get such delicious food to eat.'

For the first six months, he studied at the Ashram itself, after which he was accepted into a nearby school. He was an exceedingly diligent student. He was a bit timid, but if he saw injustice or wrongdoing, he would immediately complain about it. He once came to Sumedha ji and other seniors at the Ashram to protest something he had noticed at his school. The place didn't have proper seating arrangements or even a functional toilet; cattle entered the school premises at will. He had approached Sumedha ji because he couldn't muster up the courage to speak to the headmaster.

Around that time, we had started building Bal Mitra Grams—child-friendly villages. Here, elections for a Bal Panchayat (an elected children's council) would be held. Sumedha ji inspired schoolgoing children from the Ashram, including Om Prakash, to form a Bal Panchayat too. He won the election. Once elected, he worked alongside the other elected children to fix the issues at his school. This was his first step towards fulfilling his dreams and gave him a sense of confidence.

Before he had joined the Ashram, Om Prakash's parents had six children—four girls and two boys. To support his poverty-stricken family, he had to work in the fields owned by others. His sisters could not go to school. After living at the Ashram, he had come to understand how the effects of poverty multiply with a larger family. He resented his father for it, once, on a visit to the village, even telling him to his face that he had made a mistake by having so many children, thus making the family's circumstances worse. His father had beaten him for his audacity, and he was admonished by his mother for speaking to his father like that. A few months later, his mother gave birth to another baby girl, and two more thereafter. The seven sisters never had adequate food or clothing. Omaanku expressed his anger several times, but would be silenced by his father with a beating.

Omaanku's village was about fifteen kilometres from Bal Ashram. So he returned home during vacations at school. But he would always seem upset when he came back. He kept things bottled up, never discussing private matters at the Ashram. Although he was polite in his demeanour and as clever in conversation, he would often stutter and lie while talking about home, too ashamed to reveal domestic problems to us. The teachers would sometimes not believe him even when he spoke the truth, leading him to develop the habit of repeatedly justifying anything he said.

He had also begun stealing things to support his sisters. He loved them very much and couldn't bear to look at their condition. The dining hall of the Ashram was adjacent to the main outer wall. Om Prakash and a friend of his, Sandeep, would steal utensils and sell them over the wall. Once, he was caught doing this. Out of fear and guilt, he ran away with his friend by scaling the wall of the Ashram, but was caught by the teachers. Both the boys apologized. Happily though, after this incident, he settled into the Ashram routine. But he still didn't stop lying about home.

Om Prakash took interest in social work in his school, Bal Ashram and village. He was also very fond of playing cricket. In 2004, we undertook a historic campaign in association with renowned actress, Nandita Das. A series of cricket matches were organized to promote mutual friendship and goodwill between the children of India and Pakistan. The campaign was named 'Cricket for Peace–Peace for Cricket'. A team of Indian children was sent on a tour of Pakistan, and a team from Pakistan came on a tour to India. Mixed teams of Indian and Pakistani children were formed to play every match. Apart from the matches they played, those children spread the message of peace by participating in many socio-cultural programmes organized in schools in cities across the country. Om Prakash was among the children who visited Pakistan.

'We had been taught from our childhood in the village that Pakistan is our enemy,' he would say when he came back. 'But the people there are just like us. There was love and respect everywhere. In many places, people did not even charge us for food. There were some problems initially with our food. In our hotel, the broth that was added to the daal and vegetables was meat stock. It was our good luck that one of their own people intervened in time and stopped the person serving the food. After that, such a mistake was never repeated.'

Let me now tell you the story of how Om Prakash became Omaanku. It was the year 2005. He had accompanied me to attend some events in Japan. Just as he had once run away frightened when he first saw a television at the Ashram, he ran away in horror from the hotel door in Tokyo. There were sensors in the door. They opened automatically when someone approached them and closed when they moved away. He cried out on seeing this. We thought he was suddenly feeling unwell, or maybe he was hurt. He questioned me endlessly about the secret of those doors. He was someone who couldn't rest until he had explained his point completely, or properly understood the other's point.

The next day, we went with our hosts to meet the education minister of Japan. Some of the officers there were standing outside the building to welcome us. They greeted us by bending at the waist as is the custom in Japan. We responded in the same manner. And they bowed down again. Om Prakash, who was in the front, then bowed lower than all of them. They kept bowing down again and again instead of stopping, and so too did Om Prakash. Perhaps according to their tradition, the host must keep bowing until the guest stops. Om Prakash was so focused on returning each bow that he did not see me or our other colleagues standing behind him. He assumed that he wasn't supposed to stop till the hosts did. Eventually, one of our colleagues had to step forward to let him know he could.

Om Prakash had picked up a word or two of Japanese. He used this newly acquired linguistic skill to say hello, thank you, et cetera to anyone he met. He was totally enamoured with the wealth and splendour of Japan.

'If you had a chance,' I asked him once, 'where in the world would you like to live?'

'To tell you the truth,' he replied promptly, 'I would like to stay here.' Then he asked innocently, 'But how is that possible?'

I laughed and said, 'The easiest way is to marry a Japanese girl. You can get permission for studies and employment, but you can become a citizen of Japan only after many years.'

There was a high school student volunteering for our host organization who took great care of Omaanku. Her parents were Gujarati, but she was born in Japan. He seemed attracted to that girl. So I joked to him, 'You seem to like this girl a lot. And you are already in love with Japan. What do you say we initiate a conversation right away? In about five or six years, we could arrange for your wedding with this girl. Then you can live in Japan.'

He hung his face shyly and said, 'I'm still very young. Who will wait for so many years? This girl is three or four years older than me.'

'Don't lose heart,' I said. 'We'll get you married to some other Japanese girl. But let's give you a Japanese name for now.'

I named him Omaanku. That cheered him up. During the whole trip, that's the name everyone used for him.

Omaanku went on to achieve great success in his organizational work. It brought him to Netherlands in 2006 to receive a prestigious award given to children. He was awarded the International Children's Peace Prize on 19 November at the historic Parliament House in The Hague. The award was handed over to Omaanku by former South African president and Nobel laureate, F.W. de Klerk. Introducing Om Prakash on that occasion, he said that he was proud to present the award to a child who, along with his colleagues, had managed to get more than five hundred children registered at birth, thus giving them the recognition of being citizens of India. Omaanku spoke for the rights of children with great enthusiasm while addressing that grand assembly which consisted of many important personalities. It was a matter of great pride for me to be there.

The children brought to Bal Ashram and Mukti Ashram, rescued from slavery and trafficking, often do not know their date of birth. Neither do their illiterate parents. They make little effort to get their births registered, leaving the children with no legal identity or existence in government records. Naturally, it makes it harder for them to get admission in schools, or later, to find a job, or to acquire official documents like a passport, driving license or ration card. At that time, out of the more than twenty million born in India every year, the births of ten million children were not registered. Om Prakash had been one of them.

In 2003, our organization had launched a rigorous campaign for the birth registration of children in the districts surrounding Bal Ashram. The activists visited a large number of villages and persuaded parents to register the births of their children with the government as soon as they were born. Those who had not been registered earlier were registered too with the help of the gram panchayat (elected village council). Our workers and child leaders took part in this endeavour with great enthusiasm. Om Prakash participated actively during his holidays. He had successfully created a group of children and teenagers there, all of whom together managed to register the births of children in many villages.

That same year, our organization planned and organized the World Children's Congress in Delhi. Child leaders from forty countries of the world participated in it. Om Prakash could not leave for Delhi with the rest of the children from Bal Ashram because of a family issue. So the next day, this remarkable young lad cycled for two hundred kilometres and reached the venue on his own. He gave a very inspiring speech there about the work that he and his colleagues were doing. It was for this work that we submitted his name for the 2006 International Children's Peace Prize.

The news of the award was published prominently in many leading newspapers of Rajasthan. It was also reported that 'this award [was] accompanied by an announcement of a donation of 100,000 USD for a special children's project in the country'. After a few days, several media persons reached Om Prakash's house and interviewed his father. One of them sensed that the relationship between father and son was rather strained. That journalist badgered the father, Hariram, by asking provocative and instigating questions to make his story juicier and different from that of others. In the course of the interview, Hariram stated that he hadn't received even a single penny of the prize money, further claiming that Bal Ashram had appropriated all of it and kept his son Om Prakash hostage. The very next day that newspaper's headlines screamed, 'Where have the 45 lakhs [4.5 million] gone?' A major news piece was published with this incendiary title. It falsely stated that the prize money was given to Om Prakash.

The boy was supposed to appear for a tenth grade exam the very day this news was published. He was sad, but also angry at his father for making that statement and at the misconduct of the newspaper. He called me that day and told me between sobs that he did not have it in him to sit for the exam. I tried to persuade him but it didn't help.

Before writing the piece, the reporter had sent an inquiry to KidsRights Foundation, which had given out the award. The officials of the organization had made it clear that no money had been given to Om Prakash, Bachpan Bachao Andolan or Bal Ashram. And yet the paper had gone ahead and published the story. We were deeply anguished by it. Our detractors were quick to take advantage of this and many began to question our efforts. It was only when KidsRights sent a legal action notice to the editor of the newspaper that a clarification and revocation of the story was published.

Our Ashram hosted many international volunteers who would come and work there. Many of them were from Taiwan. The young women from Taiwan were simple and sensitive. They were warm and behaved kindly with the children and teenagers of the Ashram. I had noticed that some teenagers, including Omaanku, would meander around these volunteers, dressed in their best clothes, instead of focusing on their studies. I took Omaanku aside one day and talked at length about the changes that took place in the body during puberty and the impact of hormones on the mind and emotions of boys and girls. I told him that mutual attraction between boys and girls is a natural effect of chemical reactions taking place in the brain. I let him know that it was not unusual to fantasize about each other. Nor was that a sin. It happens to everyone after an age. But one needs to be patient, and focus one's attention on the bigger goals in life. He was a bright boy and understood what I was trying to tell him. I am happy to report that he turned his attention back to his studies.

Omaanku also had another motive for trying to get close to the foreign guests. He believed they could help his sisters with their education and maybe also provide some financial relief to his family. Having made a couple of trips abroad and met a range of different people, his self-confidence had grown tremendously. Once we had had a guest from Europe come and stay at Bal Ashram. Omaanku fostered a good friendship with this guest, a middle-aged woman. He communicated with her with the aid of a young employee who could speak English fluently. He then discreetly took the woman to his village. She was terribly moved by the pitiable condition of his family. When she returned home, she sent seven lakh rupees to help them out. This entire episode came to light when the said employee tried to siphon off all that money.

Omaanku used to collect email addresses of foreigners and send them his story. After his visits to Japan and the Netherlands, he had come to assume that all foreigners were extremely wealthy. In 2009, a young couple that had embarked on a world tour by bicycle were passing through Viratnagar. He saw them while returning from school and promptly approached them. The Dutch couple wanted to see the Sariska Tiger Reserve. So he took on the responsibility of acting as their guide and even made decent arrangements for their accommodation and sundry needs. He befriended them and they gave him a considerable amount of money. They in fact continued to do so even after they left.

He passed the twelfth grade in 2010 while living at Bal Ashram. His dream was to become a chartered accountant after pursuing a bachelor's degree in commerce. While on the one hand, he wanted, and needed, to earn a lot of money as soon as possible, on the other, he always deeply desired to work for needy and underprivileged children. He used to get the opportunity to participate in various programmes abroad through KidsRights. He would meet numerous teenagers and youth at these events striving to bring about positive change in society, which inspired him further. A dilemma brewed in Om Prakash's mind. He wanted to do social work, but the weight of his responsibilities bore heavily down on him too. That year, he and his friend, Suman Mahto, went to Delhi to pursue BCom, but were unable to secure admission there. He did get a bachelor's degree later, but in Computer Application. It was funded by KidsRights, which also assumed responsibility for the education of all his sisters until they finished high school.

Om Prakash enjoyed corresponding with his friends abroad.

To indulge his hobby while also earning a small income on the side, he started a computer typing centre and cyber café in 2010. He set it up in a locality known as Thanagazi, which happened to be close to his village. Though it wasn't a lucrative business, he was able to save a little money after managing expenses. Mona, i.e. Monika Sharma, lived near that same shop. She was in high school at the time. They quickly bonded over their shared interests, and with time, their friendship grew deeper.

'When Mona was in her mother's womb,' Omaanku once told me, 'her father had a sex determination test done. The man only wanted a son. When he came to know that there was a seven-month-old girl in the womb, he kicked his wife hard in the stomach. So the girl was born prematurely and barely survived. After that, the husband and wife were divorced. Her mother later remarried.'

'How did Mona manage to join the university you were studying in?' I asked him.

'That's also a long story,' he said. 'Those days I was doing a bachelor's degree in Computer Application in Jaipur. Mona's family couldn't afford her education after the twelfth standard. But I wanted her to study further. Arrangements had been made for the education of my sisters, but I did not have the money to send Mona to university. This was in 2014. I had gone to the Netherlands for some event. One evening I was sitting with the same friends—the cycling couple—that I had met in India. I casually told them that I had a girlfriend. I also informed them about Mona's financial status and her desire to study further. They didn't say anything at the time, but after a few days, the entire cost of Mona's admission and studies was sent directly to the university. That's how Mona could become a BCom graduate in 2017.'

Omaanku had a tender spot for small children. He was

always keen to ensure that the new children who arrived at the Ashram were taken care of with utmost attention and love. After he joined college in 2012, he began to feel particularly sorry for the children of construction workers he came across every day, malnourished and leading desultory lives. He felt a sense of responsibility to ensure that they had access to education. He set up a special programme to support these children and provide them educational opportunities in the slum area itself. Gradually, the students as well as some of the teachers in the neighbourhood started showing an interest in what he was trying to do. At the same time, along with some colleagues, Omaanku formed an organization called Paathshala. He would take sports equipment from the university and deliver it to the children. Some university officials strongly objected to this saying that he was there to study and not to take up such work. But he didn't stop. He also had the support of some of the teachers, who helped in the education of these poor and needy children.

After it was announced that I was to receive the Nobel Prize in 2014, Omaanku's interviews flooded the news. The founders of the university called him and congratulated him. He was of course not one to let such an opportunity pass. He proposed to them that he wanted to help needy children to further my work. They heartily and happily agreed. Omaanku now had four air-conditioned rooms and a computer lab to run his school. They even had projectors, among other facilities. He also started evening classes for about one hundred children. They were provided with the same sumptuous evening snack that was provided to the boarders at the school's hostel. Two buses were provided for transportation to and from the slums. By this time, Omaanku was also earning a regular income by coordinating with an international organization of youth volunteers. All these efforts had nothing to do with Bachpan Bachao Andolan. Nor was I informed about them. I was genuinely happy for him, however, and let him know it when he told me about what he had achieved. Although I could understand why some members of the organization were upset with him.

But Omaanku suffered a major setback some time after. He found out, much to his shock, that the people he had registered the school with had taken over the institution. He had faith in himself, though, and in Mona and in his friends overseas. And soon, Mona and he formed another organization named Paathshala Trust. He hopes to use the trust to continue to provide quality education to children in slums, teach handicrafts to youth as well as grown-ups and facilitate the sale of their handmade products in foreign markets.

In 2017, we had launched a nationwide march against trafficking and sexual abuse of children. Omaanku's university had taken on the responsibility of organizing the march in Jaipur.

'You can understand the situation I'm in, Bhai Sahab ji,' he said to me over a phone call after the march. 'The people of my university would always keep me in the forefront in all programmes, when often I didn't even know what the event was about. I was your dear student, after all... I couldn't get in touch with people in Bachpan Bachao Andolan...I was a bit ashamed and also afraid. But then I somehow mustered up the courage to email them. The manager of Bal Ashram was quite angry with me though and I never got a reply from him.'

He still contributed to the preparations for the march in Jaipur and even sent Mona to take part in it. She marched from Hyderabad to Delhi.

'I joined from Jaipur at Mona's behest,' he told me. 'I became very emotional when we reached Bal Ashram. I met some old friends there. When I was singing and dancing with the children,

I looked back at my own childhood. I couldn't bring myself to talk to anyone other than my old friends. Mona chided me and told me to stop acting so timid. She said I should talk to you directly. So that's what I did.'

Omaanku broke down while telling me all this. I tried to calm him down but he just said, 'Staying away from you and Bachpan Bachao Andolan for so long has been the saddest time of my life.'

He didn't stop sobbing for a long time. I then gently told him to get up and drink a glass of water first, and then make some tea for himself. We could speak after that. And so he called me after a little while.

'Have you had some tea?' I asked.

'Yes. Mona helped me relax and made me some tea,' he replied.

'It's good that you stayed away from the movement for some time,' I said, pulling his leg. 'At least you got to come close to such a nice girl. See, Mona knew that you were about to cry, so she had already started making tea! Now get married soon. After a few years, when you cry after I scold you, it won't be Mona but your children who'll try and comfort you.'

Omaanku laughed and said enthusiastically, 'Definitely, Bhai Sahab ji.'

'Do Not Think of Me as a Mere Wax Doll'

This is the story of a centuries-old effort to build towering structures above weak mud walls by laying iron ceilings over them. It is also about a struggle against that enterprise. The social institution of marriage has been set up to provide continuity, harmony, stability and permanence. There are also cultural, moral and religious foundations to this institution. This institution, however, has often been misused to tie women and children down with the shackles of slavery. This story is about breaking these shackles before they have had a chance to bind.

When seemingly ordinary girls give form to their inner strength, bravery and aspirations, they become Rajkumari, Payal, Saraswati and Deepika. Through them, a new world is born. This is their story.

Phaguni is a tiny village in the state of Bihar with a little over a couple of hundred residents living in just thirty-two houses. Getting there is not easy. To travel from Delhi or Patna to Phaguni, one has to get down at the Koderma railway station in Jharkhand, which is a neighbouring state. Koderma is the name of the station. The place one needs to first go to is 'Jhumri Tilaiya', which is ten to twelve kilometres off. The road from Koderma to Giridih takes a turn towards Neeru Pahari. From there, a crude and unpaved path leads to Phaguni. The distance from Jhumri Tilaiya to Phaguni is about fifty kilometres. This village lies in the Navada district of Bihar. Everyone in the village belongs to one of the Scheduled Castes, which are considered the lowest in the caste system. To this day, they are sometimes considered 'untouchable'.

It was 2005. I was visiting Phaguni for the first time. It was summer time. We were sitting in a crudely tiled courtyard one evening and talking to the people of the village. In the beginning there must have been a total of ten or twelve people. Soon, many women, men and children started returning from work in the mica mines. They slowly gathered around us. In our conversation with them, we learnt that all the women and men in the village had been married off at a very young age. Most of the teenagers were also married. I was explaining to them why child labour and child marriage were wrong when a young man spoke up.

'We are so poor that if the children do not work, then the family will not be able to survive at all. And if we don't get them married as children, their lives will be ruined.'

'Are you married?' I asked him gently.

'Yes,' he replied, 'I was married many years ago.'

'Where's your wife?' I then asked.

'She's often ill,' he answered despairingly. 'She has epilepsy.'

'I would like to ask all of you two things,' I said. 'First of all, how many of you have ever thought about why you are poor? And secondly, what would happen if the weight that a young man is capable of lifting on his head is placed on the head of a small child?'

For a moment, they all stared at each other. Then the same young man answered.

'We haven't thought about poverty. But yes, putting too much weight on the child's head will definitely break his neck.'

'You have answered my question correctly,' I said. 'When young girls get married, the impact on their raw minds and bodies is much more dangerous than breaking the neck. The same is happening with your wife.'

As for the first question, I answered it myself. I told them that while there were many causes of poverty, there was one crucial reason which I wanted to discuss. I spoke about how the regions of the world endowed with the most forests, mineral wealth and water had the highest number of poor and illiterate people. In the olden days, people from foreign lands went out to other countries and took their lands and resources in the name of friendship and trade, in effect, becoming their rulers. Once in power, their goal was to enslave local people, plunder all wealth, both above and below the land, and take it back to their country. As in the past, in today's era, both domestic and foreign industrialists were flocking to areas with mineral wealth and an abundance of readily available, low-cost labour. And so, the richest and most fertile lands ended up being home to the poorest people on earth. The biggest weapon to bring about change was, I suggested, education.

Some girls had been standing silently at the back of the crowd. Suddenly, one of them said, 'What's the use of girls studying? They have to go to their in-laws' house.' Saying this, she covered her face with her palms and tried to hide shyly behind her companions.

I lauded her courage for asking the question and requested everyone else to clap for her too. Then I called the girl to come and stand next to me. The girl's name was Rajkumari. She must have been ten years old. I told her that the first advantage of girls going to school was that they then don't have to leave their homes by getting married at a young age. What is more, they can also get married to educated men. There were many other advantages, like being able to choose a career for themselves. They could become teachers, doctors, engineers, lawyers, leaders, entrepreneurs, et cetera. The biggest benefit was of course that it could give them the ability to identify oppression and wrongdoing, and help them gain the courage to raise their voice against it.

Rajkumari kept looking at me with great curiosity in her eyes. Then, after some thought, she said, 'You are right. There's no school in our village. That's why my sister got married in childhood. Can you teach us?' She tried to hide her embarrassment this time by covering her face with a towel.

Her sister had been married off at the age of thirteen. She visited her maternal home from time to time. Rajkumari had been deeply troubled by what she heard about her sister's life in her in-laws' house.

Bachpan Bachao Andolan started the work of making Phaguni a Bal Mitra Gram, or child-friendly village, soon after. A school was also opened there. Dasaratha Turi's daughter, Rajkumari, was one of the first children to attend school among her peers. She was highly motivated to get children, particularly those younger than her, enrolled in the school.

There were no other means of livelihood in the village, so almost everyone worked in the mica mines. Rajkumari had also been engaged in the same work since childhood.

'We used to dig and collect *dhibra* [pieces of mica] day after day,' she tells us. 'There was no time other than night for us to play. The work in the mines would stop during heavy rainfall. That would give us a chance to play in the mud at home... There's a fair which is held every year in Pathron village, not too far from ours. I used to wait for it the whole year, because my father used to buy me a clay toy from that fair. It was difficult to preserve it for a full year. The toy would break in the middle of the year itself. That day used to be a very sad one for me.'

To be able to make it to the fair, her father had to save every penny he could. He became very angry once when she broke her toy. As she grew up and came to better appreciate the struggle her parents went through, Rajkumari had given up insisting on that yearly gift. To aid the family's income, she had started working in the mica mines herself.

About five years after we began our work in Phaguni village, in the year 2010, Bachpan Bachao Andolan had organized a 'National Bal Mahapanchayat' (national children's megacouncil) at Gandhi Sansthan, Rajghat in Delhi. It was attended by nearly two hundred child representatives from the Bal Mitra Grams, from twelve states across the country, with exciting and inspiring stories of their struggles and achievements.

Our esteemed chief guest Justice Dr M.K. Sharma, a senior judge of the Supreme Court of India, graced the stage along with some young leaders. Justice Sharma was warm and friendly with the children, who felt comfortable confiding in him. Rajkumari from Phaguni was one of them.

'I was the first person in my village to hold a pen and paper,' she proudly said to him. 'The activists from Bachpan Bachao

Andolan explained to us what a Bal Mitra Gram was. We all liked what they said it would be like. My father also agreed that instead of working as a labourer, I should be educated. Gradually, our village has become a child-friendly village. This means that almost all the children in the village have been taken out of child labour and enrolled in school.'

'Were the parents of all children convinced easily?' Justice Sharma asked.

'No,' Rajkumari replied promptly, 'like all the other men, my father used to stop by at the local alcohol stand while returning from the mica mine. He would consume it and come home heavily drunk. My mother never said anything when he abused her, and sometimes even beat her up. My brothers and I felt very bad. But we kept quiet out of fear. After the work of the Bal Mitra Gram started, many children and their mothers started speaking up against alcoholism. Then the workers brought the women of the village together and formed a Mahila Mandal [Women's Group]. Similarly, a Yuva Mandal [Youth Group] was formed. The women and youth groups were involved in spreading awareness about all kinds of issues in the village. Gradually, the effect of their advice could be seen across the whole village. Initially, most people were not happy that we were asking children to give up work to study in the school. Everyone used to say that it was futile to educate a girl. She should get married soon! But my friends and I did not bow down to those people.'

Then Justice Sharma asked her a different question: 'What has been your happiest moment till now?'

After giving it a little thought, she replied, 'I would have been able to answer that if there was just one moment of happiness.'

'All right, then! Tell us all of them,' he said.

'The first time I drew some circles on the paper with my pencil,' she answered, 'Masterji said, "What have you drawn?" I told him that I had drawn a roti. He said to me it was also the moon. It really excited me. I realized that education could enable us to do anything we want. If we are educated, we can earn a good living for ourselves, live with dignity, and even reach the moon. Then I was the really happy when I was elected the leader in the Bal Panchayat [children's council] election.'

'So tell us what will make you even happier?' I asked her.

'The day I go to class as a teacher,' was the immediate reply.

'Why teacher?' I asked.

'Bhai Sahab ji,' she said, 'when all the children study and read and write inside the classroom, only then will child labour and child marriage stop. And who else but a teacher will educate them?'

Rajkumari continued her education, but after some time her family began talking about getting her married. She was about fifteen years old now. Her family had, in fact, even finalized the groom. But Rajkumari objected and simply refused to go ahead with the marriage. It led to a big quarrel at home. She almost got beaten up for her disobedience, but she did not give in. She told the workers of the Bal Mitra Gram that they had better convince her father or she would complain to the police. The matter was somehow resolved and the marriage was called off. This was the first time in Rajkumari's village, and in fact many villages of that region, when a girl had protested and put a stop to her own marriage. Few were unaware of the incident. Slowly, our campaign against child labour and child marriage gained momentum across the entire mica mining region. Most importantly, it was led by the children themselves, who set examples of bravery by preventing their own marriages.

Before Bihar and Jharkhand, we had been working for some time on creating child-friendly villages in Rajasthan. Hundreds of children in these villages had come together to bring about an end to child labour and child marriage in their region. One of them was Payal Jangid, who shines like a star today. She was very proactive in the campaign to make her village, Hinsla, a child-friendly village. She was thus elected the head of her Bal Panchayat in 2013. She was eleven years old at the time. Payal's father worked as a carpenter, and she helped him with his work. For a girl to win an election against a group of boys was no less than a revolution for this region. But there was really no reason for this truthful and fearless girl, always willing to help others, to not win the contest.

One day, she came to know that preparations for her marriage, and that of her thirteen-year-old sister, were underway. They were to be married to two brothers from a neighbouring village. As the Bal Panchayat chief, committed to raising awareness against child marriage, Payal could not let this happen. She confronted her parents, letting them know that she would neither marry nor allow her sister to be married. There was a fierce clash of wills at her home that day.

Child marriages and female foeticide were rampant in and around Hinsla and few, if any, of the girls were even literate. In many cases, marriages were arranged even before the birth of the children. Sometimes distant relatives would promise their children in marriage to each other if one of them had a son and the other a daughter.

Payal's family was determined to go ahead with the wedding, and Payal was adamant about not getting married. The elders of the house and close relatives were trying to browbeat her emotionally. Her parents told her that it would become impossible for them to live honourably within the community if she refused. Payal threatened to file a complaint with the police, but they were unrelenting. She finally shared her problem with her Bal Panchayat colleagues and the workers of the Bal Mitra Gram, asking for their cooperation and help. Sumedha ji and the manager of Bal Ashram, Adesh Sharma, came to her aid. They reasoned with Payal's father and family members to call the marriage off. They argued that it would be better for both Payal and her family in the long run. Since the matter had been dragging for some time, the news could not be contained within the household. It reached the family of the boys the sisters were supposed to wed. They were horrified and went to Hinsla to break the arrangement off themselves, declaring that they would never marry their sons to such impudent girls.

That chapter was over, but Payal had become infamous in the community. It became difficult for her father to face the villagers and even his own kin. He would be chided everywhere he went for having committed the so-called sin of sending her daughter to school which had made her a free thinker. On the other hand, the news of Payal's bravery had spread far and wide. She was felicitated by the Bal Panchayat, her school and Bal Ashram. She had become a role model for many such girls who were faced with a life shackled by marriage. Along with her Bal Panchayat, Payal not only made her own village but also many surrounding ones free from child marriages. News of her laudable acts had started appearing in the newspapers and the wise people of the Jangid community began to show her due respect.

She used to visit the Ashram frequently to participate in the joint activities of the various child-friendly villages. She would be actively involved in programmes held in Delhi and other places. I therefore met her often.

'A few days back,' she once told me with great enthusiasm, 'the sub-divisional magistrate of our locality came to my house. He was accompanied by many officers, policemen and media persons. My neighbours were scared. Perhaps they thought that

I had either done something wrong or someone had complained against my father. But all those officers had come to meet and congratulate me. They were insisting that I campaign against child marriage on behalf of the government in Alwar district.'

'That's great!' I said. 'What did you say then?'

'I told them that we have freed all the children of our village from child labour and enrolled them in school,' she said. 'But the condition of the school is quite bad. Our skills are not up to the mark. We don't even have enough teachers. Government schemes meant for the poor, the elderly and women are not implemented properly in our village. Please look into all this first, sir. I will consult with the senior colleagues of the organization and tell you then whether we can work together with the government or not. They agreed to do what I had requested. And after talking to Adesh Bhaiya and the others, I too said yes.'

I congratulated her. She had understood well that social issues cannot not be isolated from each other. There is indeed a deep connection, I told her, between social security, development, human rights and the eradication of crime. I then added in jest, 'It seems that you'll soon be elected sarpanch of the gram panchayat instead of the Bal Panchayat.'

'What are you saying?' she cut me off. 'You're the one who keeps telling us that if one has the freedom to dream, one shouldn't dream small. One should dream big. Then why should I dream of becoming a sarpanch?'

'Sorry,' I said, 'I forgot. You must dream of becoming the prime minister. But still, there's no harm getting elected as a sarpanch as the first step.'

She laughed at that. But after a moment of thought, she said, 'What you just mentioned about social security and crime, I did not understand that well. Please explain that.'

I made her and the other children sit beside me on the platform built under the neem tree in the Ashram.

'The children who had been freed from child labour,' I asked all of them, 'how were you able to easily get admission in school?'

One child replied, 'That was their right, because we have the RTE [Right to Education Act] in our country.'

'Is there any benefit from the mid-day meal provided in the school?' I asked again.

Two or three children said together, 'Yes, it definitely is beneficial... Earlier, our parents and even we used to think that we can earn some money by working. Now, we enjoy going to school for the free food, along with the classes.'

When I asked the children how many of their parents received the benefit of the government's rural employment guarantee scheme, many children raised their hands. They said that their parents worked as labourers building roads and dams, digging ponds and installing electric poles under this scheme.

Then I asked them whether this scheme had had a role to play in helping them go to school instead of working. They admitted that the families who were getting the benefit of such schemes wanted their children to study further.

'Programmes like mid-day meals and employment guarantees,' I then explained to them, 'are called social security. Building roads and dams are works of development. Child labour and child marriage are legal offences. Education is a fundamental right.'

Payal and all the other children were thrilled by this lesson. 'Now I've understood that we have to work on all the issues together,' she said.

Pappu Ram Jangid had begun to realize that his daughter, Payal, was special. Newspapers continued to publish stories about her, and there were constant visits by government officials to their home and an ever-increasing number of admirers. Previously, he had believed his daughter to be defiant, stubborn and proud, but when the villagers started to show her respect, he too began to respect her. And then, a few years later, he himself started supporting his daughter's efforts to fight child marriage. The Jangid community calls Payal the pride of their community.

In 2015, the president of the United States, Barack Obama, along with First Lady Michelle Obama, visited India as the chief guest for the Republic Day celebrations on 26 January. I had a personal meeting with him during the visit. Sumedha ji and I had taken along Deepak, a child rescued from agricultural bonded labour, and also Payal. These children were symbols of human freedom, dignity and hope. We introduced them to the Obamas. Michelle Obama cares deeply about adolescent girls and their issues. She was moved by Payal's story. She took off the ring she was wearing on her finger and put it on Payal's finger. We were rather surprised, including President Obama. Payal thanked her and returned the white gold, diamond-studded ring.

'Madam,' she said, 'maybe this is your wedding ring. I can't keep it. If you want to give me a gift, then promise me that the next time you come to India, you will definitely visit my village.'

Michelle Obama embraced Payal and showed great affection for the young girl. She promised to visit her village.

Along with Payal's fame, her efforts towards protecting children's rights also grew. She was invited to Stockholm to serve as a jury member for the International Children's Rights Award in Sweden. She met many influential figures at the event, including the Queen of Sweden. Her passion and grit, born of her personal life and struggle in eliminating child marriage, inspired many.

The year 2019 was one of pride not only for Payal, but for our movement and the nation as a whole. On the evening of 25 September, the now seventeen-year-old Payal made history as the first Indian to receive the prestigious Changemaker

Award by the Bill and Melinda Gates Foundation at the grand Goalkeepers Global Goals Awards event in New York. Payal Jangid was presented with the award by Amina Mohammed, deputy secretary-general of the United Nations, in the presence of Bill and Melinda Gates and other notable figures from around the globe. Prime Minister Narendra Modi too was honoured with an award on the same stage.

Sumedha ji and I were present in the audience. Payal's dignified, graceful and humble presence on that magnificent stage cast a spell over the entire auditorium, which erupted in thunderous applause at almost every line of her speech. At the end, she received a standing ovation. We were thrilled, happy and proud. She was mobbed for selfies and photographs after the ceremony was over, by media persons and others who wanted to congratulate her, so we were only able to get back to our hotel very late in the night. After Payal returned to her village, she was honoured by several social organizations as well as the administration for her efforts. Today, she is not only pursuing a bachelor's degree, but continues to fight for the rights of children.

In 2013, Rajkumari was married to boy in a village called Markachho, seventy kilometres from Phaguni. She was about nineteen years old. Her husband used to work as a labourer in Mumbai. Rajkumari spent most of her time looking after her old in-laws. I could speak with her only once in a while on the phone. She was happy in her in-laws' house, but she complained about not being able to do social work any more. She fervently longed to join Bachpan Bachao Andolan as an activist. Three years after their marriage, she finally told her husband about her desire to be involved in the movement. But he rebuked her and refused her request.

However, Rajkumari was not one to keep quiet. She warned her husband and in-laws that if they did not allow her, she would go ahead anyway and do what she knew was the right thing to do.

'Do not think of me as a mere wax doll,' she warned them sternly.

Her husband was quite angry and upset and that put a strain on their relationship. But despite the opposition she faced at home, Rajkumari continued to fight for the education of girls and the eradication of child labour. In her own small way, she was determined to make a difference.

She remained in touch with the workers of the child-friendly villages and kept insisting that she wanted to go back to her maternal village and fulfil her dream of becoming a teacher. Finally, in 2019, our organization welcomed her back to the same school where she had studied, this time as a teacher. Today, she is a proud mother of two girls. One of them is five years old and the other is two. I recently spoke to her on the phone after many years and she was ecstatic to hear my voice.

'Sir, I have become a teacher,' she said.

'Rajkumari, do you know who you are talking to?' I interrupted her.

'Yes, sir,' she replied, a little nervously, 'I know. I'm talking to Shri Kailash Satyarthi ji.'

'Tell me,' I asked, 'when have you ever called me "Sir" before? And who taught you to speak like this?'

She felt embarrassed and immediately corrected herself. 'No, Bhai Sahab ji,' she said, 'sorry. This was a mistake. Here in the meetings and in the school, they call each other as "Sir ji" and "Madam ji". Everyone uses "Sir" all the time.'

'Well, your father is much older than you...' I joked, 'have you started calling him "Sir" too?'

'I won't make this mistake again, Bhai Sahab ji.'

Rajkumari sounded happy and proud of herself that day. 'Dreams don't come true without hard work,' she said. 'I had always dreamed of becoming a teacher, but given the state of our home, it seemed almost impossible. Now, I am respected by all. Every girl and boy in the village has the opportunity to attend school.'

'Now your dream has come true, child,' I said. 'Take care of your family as well and make sure your daughters are educated and become good human beings like you.'

'It's not that simple, Bhai Sahab ji. My struggles are still not over. My daughters' father and grandparents are very unhappy with me. They keep complaining that I don't have a son. I'm now financially independent and live in my maternal home, but I make sure to visit my in-laws every fortnight. Still, they all seem to despise me and my choices,' she lamented. 'But...do you remember that slogan you taught us?'

'I had taught you many slogans. Remind me, which one are you talking about, child?'

She said: '*Ladenge, jeetenge! Hum ladke lenge azadi, hum chheen ke lenge azadi! Humein jaan se pyaari azadi!*' (We will fight, we will win! We will fight for freedom, and achieve it! Freedom is dearer to us than life itself!)

I was deeply moved by Rajkumari's words.

'Am I Still a Little Child?'

This is the story of the countless girls who die every day, one of whom was fourteen-year-old Bhavna, who despised the sight of the beast called Man. This is the story of a flower that is plucked if it withers, and plucked if it blooms.

But rightly said the poet: 'Durbal ko na sataiye, jaki moti haay / Mari khaal ki saans se, loh bhasam ho jaaye.' (Do not oppress the poor and weak, believing them to be helpless. Remember that the breath of the lifeless blower can turn iron to ashes.) Bhavna let out her tiny voice in a small local court, but it reverberated in the highest courts of the country. This is the story of the echo of that voice, which not only changed the lives of innumerable children, but also the law of the land.

I will never be able to forget that day I sat talking to Bhavna in the gol kutiya of Mukti Ashram in Delhi.

This thatched hut, open on all sides, in the centre of the Ashram stands tall on eight sturdy wooden pillars. Up to fifty or sixty children can be seated there. Thousands of children have experienced liberation for the first time in their lives there. After years of servitude and oppression, that shelter helped them reclaim their childhood. After years, they could have an identity of their own, find their voice, gain self-confidence and feel a sense of humanity. We built a similar hut at Bal Ashram in Rajasthan as well.

She was a dusky girl with a round face, around fourteen or fifteen years old. I can still recall my conversation with her that day. Her real name isn't Bhavna, but I refer to her as such to keep her identity concealed. Tears were streaming down Bhavna's sorrowful face that day.

'You people are fortunate; you only die once in life,' she said. 'I have died every day. I have died a hundred deaths. I cannot even count how many times I've died.'

There was a hint of reproach and rage in her voice, yet not an ounce of defeat. Her face was flushed with anger. She held the legs of her chair tightly with both her hands, as if their support gave her the courage to speak. Or like she wanted to vent her fury on them.

An awkward silence hung in the air. I could find no words to comfort her. Then I got up and brought two glasses of water from the kitchen. She took one in her hand and began to sob uncontrollably. I drank some from my glass and gently urged her to do the same. Each teardrop that fell into her glass felt like a drop of blood making its way down my skin, trickling from somewhere deep within me. After a few tentative sips of water, she resumed talking, without me having asked her anything.

'If we let fear show on our face while doing dangerous tricks,' she said, 'or if we made any mistake, we were punished at night. If we kept smiling, jumping from one swing to the other or standing on the trunk of an elephant, the owner would jeer and say, "You were looking very sexy today." He used to reward us for it. But don't ask me what the punishment was, or for that matter, the reward. They were both the same. After the shows were over, the owner or his men would storm into our beds like ravenous wolves. If this isn't death, then what is?'

I could see how much strength Bhavna had had to muster up to say this. Her lips and nostrils were trembling. My hands and feet were shaking with anger too. I was grinding my teeth and clenching my fists. But the strain from even that slight movement upset the bandages that covered my head, back and legs, making the wounds hurt. Bhavna knew that I had been grievously injured in the attacks by the circus owners while freeing her and the twenty-three girls with her.

It was the month of June in 2004. The parents of some girls came to our office one day. They were from different villages of the Hetauda district of Nepal. Bhavna's mother, Vishumala, was among them. Hetauda is a very backward and poor area of western Nepal, bordering the Gorakhpur district of Uttar Pradesh in India. Nepal and India share a long and intertwined history, and have maintained strong cultural, religious and economic ties since ancient times. The two countries today have an open border, with few restrictions on the movement or domicile of their citizens. This means that no passport or visa is required for travel between the two countries.

This small but beautiful and mountainous country is bordered to its north by another of the world's great powers, China. Both of these powers have a huge influence on Nepal's politics, society and economy. Yet Nepal is one of the poorest countries in the world. More than four million expatriate Nepalese live in India. In fact, since the British period, six 'Gorkha regiments' have been serving in the Indian Army, which draw their troops from the ethnic Gurkhas, a warrior community that lives in Nepal and India, renowned for their loyalty and bravery. Apart from their long history of service in the Indian Army, they have also served in the British and American armies. A number of Nepali people have also found employment as domestic workers here. But there is also large-scale trafficking of Nepali girls to Indian brothels, with estimates of their current numbers ranging from three to four hundred thousand. Apart from being cheap, they are preferred by brothel owners because of their fair complexion and physical appearance.

Thousands of women and girls trafficked from Nepal for prostitution live in notorious brothel areas like GB Road in Delhi, Sonagachi in Calcutta and Kamathipura in Mumbai. Apart from the adults, it is the young boys of the household who migrate to India or the Gulf countries in search of a source of income. Living on their own, the young girls that are left behind become all the more vulnerable. The pimps keep an eye out for such girls to traffic them into a life of exploitation.

Among the parents who came to us was a man named Mahendranath. Mahendra worked in Lucknow in Uttar Pradesh. He was there when his seven-year-old daughter, who lived in the village back home in Nepal, was taken by the traffickers. Luring them with the promise of a good income, the pimp had trafficked girls to India previously as well. Vishumala lived in a neighbouring village. She was an impoverished widow who somehow managed to eke out a living for herself and her only daughter, eight-year-old Bhavna. That pimp had assured the parents of the girls that he would take them to India and get them work in the circus, where they would earn a lot of money.

'The circus agent gave me two thousand rupees to get my thumb impression on some blank papers,' Vishumala told us. 'My daughter used to study in grade one but due to the Maoists there, the school was closed for several months and was being used as a police camp. That's why Bhavna had to discontinue her education. I was reluctant to give her to that man, but when I saw that other people from the village were doing the same, I was convinced by the man's promise and agreed. After her father's death, my family was in financial hardship and we couldn't even afford to buy clothes. I had hoped that with her own earnings, my daughter's condition would improve and I would be able to arrange a good marriage for her. I had informed the man that my daughter wanted to study. He told me that the circus activities took place only in the evenings. He even assured me that the circus provided a safe and secure environment for children and that Bhavna would be able to continue her studies too. He added that the circus also provided healthy snacks and meals for the performers.'

She kept wiping her tears again and again as she shared this. She then said, 'My daughter is ruined. Please save her, sir.'

Vishumala was speaking in Nepali. I could understand most of what she said. Vikram, a Nepali worker in our office, helped me with the rest even though he would, at times, become emotional himself and unable to continue speaking.

Determined to find their daughters, the parents had searched high and low, visiting many circuses in India. Their hope dwindled with each passing day. They had no clue where their children might be trapped. But they did not give up. Some time back, a Nepali youth had somehow escaped from a circus named 'Great Roman' and gone back to his village in Hetauda. The parents learnt from him that about two dozen girls from the district performed in the same circus. The girls faced numerous atrocities daily. Coincidentally, the parents had also met some people whose children we had rescued from the 'Great Indian Circus' a few months ago. They had informed Vishumala and Mahendra about Bachpan Bachao Andolan. An organization which worked for child welfare in Hetauda had helped the parents connect with us.

In 2002, we had started a vigorous campaign to eradicate child slavery from the circuses in India. A team of young people under the leadership of Rajiv Bhardwaj, Bhuwan Ribhu and Vinay Singh Lanu was involved in that work. During this campaign, some people from the same Hetauda district had approached us. Their children were being kept captive in 'King Bharat Circus' for the past six to ten years. They had visited India several times in search of their children, only to learn that King Bharat Circus had closed years ago. Someone had told them that before they close their business, circuses sell their child performers to other circuses at high rates. The better the 'artist', the higher their price.

When they investigated the matter, our workers found that 'King Bharat Circus' had changed its name to 'Great Indian Circus'. At the time, it was running a show in a town called Shoranur in Kerala. The raid and rescue operation was conducted by the team led by Rajiv Bhardwaj on 17 April 2004. They were accompanied by the parents of the children, the police and the local magistrate.

During the raid, one man ran impatiently ahead of all others.

Desperate to find his daughter, Ramu Bahadur was losing his mind. When he had handed over nine-year-old Basanti to a circus recruiter for a small sum of money, he had not imagined that his longing to see her would last ten years. Within minutes of entering the circus, they found a bunch of boys and girls, but Ramu's eyes were searching only for Basanti. She was there among the children, but Ramu couldn't recognize her. When she was separated from her parents, she was fair and slim, like a little doll in a frock, but she had become a plump young woman now with a dusky complexion and a face marked with pimples.

After a few moments, as soon as he recognized Basanti, he rushed towards her with a heart-wrenching cry.

'She is my daughter.'

But the girl remained silent. Her face was strangely expressionless.

'Is this your father?' the magistrate present there asked her.

She kept staring at Ramu with wide-open eyes. After a while, she shook her head, but still said nothing.

Ramu was crying. 'Daughter, I'm your father.'

'No,' she bellowed, when asked again.

Then, abruptly, she began to laugh out loud. Everyone was taken aback. All the other children had recognized their parents. Tears of joy streamed down their faces as they embraced each other.

The magistrate and Rajiv were confused. So they took some children aside and inquired about Basanti.

'Sir,' Mona, a friend of Basanti, said, 'she is lying out of fear. The circus manager, seeing the police approaching, had threatened all of us not to tell the truth. Not only this, the guard of the circus had put a gun to Basanti's temple and told her that if she identified her father, he would shoot both of them... Basanti has been treated very cruelly for many years. We've never seen her smiling or laughing. But just a while ago, when she saw her father entering the gate, she started rolling on the ground in pure joy. Then she clung to me. She was crying but kept saying out loud, "Buba! Buba!" [Father! Father!] At that moment, the guard came towards us and pointed his gun at her. She began to shake uncontrollably.'

The magistrate was convinced that the girl was indeed Ramu's daughter. She was now free, but having lived through unimaginable trauma, she had lost control of her mental faculties. She would sometimes wail and at other times burst into loud laughter. A doctor was quickly summoned and he gave Basanti some sleeping pills among other medication. The thirty children thus rescued were then brought to Mukti Ashram in Delhi.

At the Ashram, Basanti was shown to a psychiatrist, who said that she was probably unable to process her emotions, the simultaneous feeling of immense fear and elation upon reuniting with her father after a decade. It had disturbed her mental equilibrium. While he assured us that she would recover, he also informed us that the treatment would take time. We kept everyone at Mukti Ashram for a few days before sending them safely back to Nepal.

Vishumala, along with the others, had found out about us from Ramu Bahadur, and so, she had absolute faith in us. The 'Great Roman Circus', in which their daughters worked, was then currently in Karnailganj in Uttar Pradesh. As soon as we received this information, a group of activists was dispatched to the location. Having already conducted extensive research into circuses, we were aware that Fateh Khan and his son, Raza Khan, were the proprietors of this circus. Fateh Khan owned several other circuses, and it was rumoured that he had taken possession of one of them after killing one of his relatives. He was a notorious mafia kingpin with immense influence in the politics of Uttar Pradesh. He allegedly trafficked drugs, illicit weapons and women into India under the pretext of running a circus business.

The bigger the canopy used for the circus events and for seating the spectators, the greater the space it needs for its animals and workers to camp on. It takes many large lorries and trucks to transport the circus paraphernalia from one place to another. The entire show runs like a huge machine, of which every human and animal is a cog. It must keep moving without any glitches. There is no place in the circus for the sick, injured, disabled or elderly stuntmen, artists and animals. They are only tolerated for a few months before being unfeelingly discarded when the circus has wrung them dry. No one cares as these helpless people wither and die in the dark of obscurity. They include girls who have become pregnant due to rape or lack of proper precaution.

A woman who used to work in a circus once told me, 'Apart from animal feed and grocery items, body paint and contraceptive pills are the most widely used products in our circuses. We underwent regular check-ups; not for diseases of the lungs, nose, ear or mouth, but only that of the abdomen. Of course, no one knew whether the unborn child belonged to the teacher, the owner, the manager or the special guests at new locations... We knew we wouldn't be hired even to clean their toilets when we grew old. So we always prayed that God took us before we grew old and useless.'

The young girls in the circus were closely watched by those who had become the 'courtesans' of the proprietors, administrators and other managers. In exchange, they would receive stylish clothing, good food and money. Despite living together, all the performers remained divided due to mutual rivalry, enmity and suspicion.

But it was not as if only predators lived in this hell. Occasionally, a master of animals, say, would oppose the brutal treatment of innocent children by the junior staff. When such a person treats the animals cruelly by beating or starving them, it is often the case that he is himself living under humiliation and distress, an indication of the corruption at the top.

During the raid at Karnailganj, the behaviour of the government employees, the police and even the magistrate was highly dubious. It was fairly clear that they were in collusion with the owner of the circus. By the time we reached, the girls had already been hidden. As soon as we entered, Fateh Khan's son, Raza Khan, pulled out a pistol, and in a fit of rage, pointed it straight at me. I managed a narrow escape from the circus tent, but as soon as we came out to the main road, we were viciously attacked by their goons. The parents of two girls, our youth activist, Govind Khanal, my son, Bhuwan, and I were severely injured in the assault. Bhuwan and I were taken in a press car to a hospital in Lucknow, where we were admitted in a critical state.

But one good happened during the commotion. A companion of mine, who had been left behind at the circus, noticed a spot where a herd of elephants had been crowded together. A little girl sat crouching near that spot to protect herself. That girl was Bhavna. She had seen her mother during the raid, but had run to that area and hid out of fear.

Two of our colleagues cautiously approached her. 'We have come here with your parents,' they said. 'We have come here to set you free.'

At first, she tried to run away, but in the hope of reaching her mother, she followed them. They tried to leave through the toilet area, but were spotted by the circus staff, who ran towards them and forcibly dragged Bhavna away.

Our workers managed to hide and then escape into the

surrounding fields. From there, they saw a big car filled with young girls exiting the circus. One of the girls was frantically shouting, 'Save me! Save me!' She was desperately trying to climb out of the window, her body half hanging out of it. It appeared that someone inside was holding her legs and pulling her back. The car moved slowly through the fields. One of our workers took advantage of that fact, ran up to the car and dragged the girl off. It was the same girl they had found hiding by herself at the circus. He ran with her in the opposite direction to the car. Those inside it perhaps did not want to stop and waste time, because they kept going.

The three of them ran towards the road, where they were confronted by some police constables. They pushed our colleagues away and forcibly took the howling child to the police station, where she was locked inside a cell. Our workers followed them there, but they were not allowed to meet her. We were at the hospital in Lucknow being treated for our injuries when I found out about all this a few hours later. After receiving the necessary treatment, Vishumala was promptly sent to Karnailganj. A few of our other colleagues reached the police station to help her lodge a complaint. Despite a lot of effort, the police refused to let her meet Bhavna. An injured Bhuwan and a few of our other lawyers contacted the district superintendent of police to express their misgivings regarding this matter. Consequently, the mother was granted permission to meet her daughter.

Vishumala was delirious when she met her daughter. It had been six years since she had last seen her. Our colleagues argued with the inspector that, legally, Bhavna could not be detained. She ought to be given back to her mother, since she was the victim, not the perpetrator. But they had to return to Lucknow without Bhavna. Vishumala, however, refused to leave her daughter alone at the police station, and so, she lay herself down at a spot outside the lock-up itself. After the constable departed, the other policemen left her lying there and retired for the night.

That evening was an important one. It would go on to shape the character and future of the entire circus industry in India. My son, Bhuwan, and I were trying to pass the night in excruciating pain in Lucknow, while at the police station in Karnailganj, Bhavna shed her inhibitions and revealed the entire truth to her mother across the bars of the cell.

She told her that Raza Khan, the circus manager and his men had sexually assaulted her many times. For her, performing 'shows' in the circus during the day and tolerating their abuse at night had become the routine. She had also had an abortion when she was fourteen years old. She told her mother that the night before, most of the girls had been made to disappear by the police and Raza Khan. The remainder were forced into a car and driven to an unknown location.

The next morning, our colleagues reached Karnailganj again, to get Bhavna released. A female activist spoke to her to find out if she would be willing to tell the truth in court. Her resolve was strong as steel. She immediately agreed. On the advice of Bhuwan, a local lawyer filed an appeal to the court that the custody of the girl be transferred to her mother. Legal action was demanded against Raza Khan and others. But our application was not heard that day. Our appeal was slotted for the following day. Vishumala remained in the waiting area of the police station.

The incident of the raid and rescue operation was repeatedly shown on many big TV news channels. The details were published on the front pages of all major newspapers. Yet there was no indication of any action being taken by the government. Meanwhile, Raza Khan's father, Fateh Khan, had gone to

Karnailganj with his men to help his son. There wasn't a spot in that small town—including the police station, the court, the markets and lawyers' offices—that goons in cars and on motorcycles did not rake through looking for our activists, trying to instil fear. When our team went to Karnailganj the following morning to try again to get Bhavna out of the lock-up, they found the same men sitting in the police station's yard, drinking alcohol and feasting on chicken. By then, Bhavna and Vishumala had repeatedly been threatened by people from the circus and police. They had even tried to bribe them with thousands of rupees. The mother and daughter did not say a word then. They just listened. They only broke their silence in the court of law.

With immense courage, the minor girl had made a grave allegation against Raza Khan and others, accusing them of repeatedly raping her. The judge adjourned the hearing for a few days after ordering a medical examination. He also ordered for the girl to be kept in the women's jail. This was grossly illegal and our lawyers vehemently argued against it. But the judge did not agree.

Eventually, despite attempts by the circus mafia to intimidate and buy the doctors off, rape was confirmed in the medical report. The senior doctor of the government hospital was apparently willing to write a false report, but an honest female doctor was determined to stand for the truth. Which finally came to light, and Raza Khan was arrested and locked up. The policemen kept busy late into the night making luxury arrangements for their 'royal guest' in the lock-up. He was provided with a comfortable bed, a television, a sofa set, mineral water, fruits and more. Additionally, generators were installed to ensure that there was no inconvenience due to power cuts. His men had already arranged for good food and expensive liquor, two mobile phones and clothes, among other things, at the station for him. The 'five-star' hospitality provided by the police was even featured in the local newspapers.

In the following hearing, the judge ordered that Vishumala submit certain documents to the court for the approval of Bhavna's bail, such as a government ID, property papers, the girl's birth certificate and evidence of Vishumala's relationship to Bhavna. It came as a bolt out of the blue. Our lawyers were equally perplexed at the mention of these documents. Poor, illiterate Vishumala, who used to tend to goats in a remote Nepalese village, had never heard of such papers before. How were we to explain to the learned judge that had Bhavna's mother been literate and able, her daughter would not have been forced into slavery in India? More than half of the Nepali population did not have birth registration certificates, and a proof of identity was rarer still. And so, with the date fixed for her next court appearance, Bhavna remained in prison.

On that day, one of our local friends had to provide surety to the court for Bhavna to be released. She felt confident after being let out. The girl had an extraordinary memory. She provided information about the names and whereabouts of numerous individuals, who were suspected to be hiding the other girls. This important information was passed on to the senior officers of Lucknow Police, and later proved to be very useful.

We felt a huge sense of relief when the Uttar Pradesh High Court accepted our petition and issued notices to the state government. In the very first hearing, the judge directed a number of senior government officials and the state's director general of police to locate and liberate the girls mentioned in the petition. As a result, twenty-four girls were freed, even though only twelve parents had come to us with complaints. After the paperwork in Lucknow, the girls and their parents were taken to Delhi and lodged at Mukti Ashram.

I met her the next morning. I was proud of her courage and integrity. I used to imagine what her face would look like. In my mind, I had conjured up a face that looked like my daughter, Asmita. I settled down in the gol kutiya once I arrived at Mukti Ashram. Upon seeing the bandages on my wounds, the children and workers of the Ashram began to cry. The freed Nepali girls also came and sat there, but Bhavna was not among them. After some time, Vishumala came with her daughter. I had the urge to hug and express the tenderness I felt for her, but I held back. She seemed shy and scared. Vishumala began to sob, but with a little consolation, she went ahead and seated herself on a chair. Bhavna stood in silence a little distance behind her mother, her head lowered. I had been told that she did not like to talk to men, let alone see them. Apart from delivering her testimony in court, she had not uttered a single word to any male. I completely understood her hatred and rage for men, and yet I was conflicted and felt a peculiar unease.

I felt better when Bhavna eventually joined the other girls in the corner. To lighten the mood, I attempted to make the children laugh. I would glance at her every now and then, but she never looked up. She kept her eyes glued to the ground, scratching the earth with her feet, her head bowed. Almost an hour passed. I noticed the children in front of me readjusting themselves and realized that she had slowly made her way behind me.

Without turning to look back, I started narrating the story of Bhavna's bravery. I said that she would soon go back to her village and resume her studies, and by studying, she would become a well-educated woman. She would be able to enjoy nutritious meals and buy good clothes. Once she gets married, she would go to her in-laws' house as a bride. And even a mother-in-law will not be able to trouble an educated daughter-in-law!

Pointing towards Vishumala, I asked if she would return to Nepal and send her daughter to school.

'Yes, Bhai Sahab,' she replied, 'I'll do as you say.'

'Just tell me,' I insisted, 'will you send her to study again?'

'Yes, I will definitely send her to study,' she said.

Just then, I felt a gentle, loving touch on my right arm. It was Bhavna. All the children sitting in front stared at her, yet she seemed to not notice. She slowly caressed my shoulder and hand. I became very emotional, but I kept my composure, speaking about trivial topics. Eventually, I heard her whisper.

'How can I go to school? I am a grown-up now. Am I still a little child?'

I extended my hand to invite her to sit next to me, but then stopped myself. I simply asked her to sit, which she did. But then I couldn't help myself and reached out and gently placed one hand on her head, lifting her chin with the other so she was facing me.

'Yes, daughter,' I said, 'of course you are still very much a child. Which fool says you're a grown-up?'

Bhavna's eyes looked into mine. I felt her cold stare probing me with a thousand unspoken questions that lay frozen inside her. Suddenly, she stood up from her seat and embraced me tightly. She didn't hold back her tears as she wept. She kept crying for some time, as if the skies had crumbled, and the sun had melted the icy layers of her questions, and they were cascading down as tears. I made her sit back down on the chair, giving her sips of water.

Bhavna held on to my hand tightly and said, 'I cannot remember my father's face. I feel like you are my father.'

Her tears were dripping onto my other palm, and some of my own may have fallen on her face. None of the children or elders in attendance could contain their emotions either. The entire place was filled with the sound of people crying. Most of them had covered their eyes and faces with their palms. I started cracking some jokes again a little while later. Bhavna sat next to me, still holding my hand. After some time, I asked everyone to leave the gol kutiya except Vishumala, so only the three of us remained.

'Daughter, tell me. What do you want to be when you grow up?' I asked Bhavna.

'I don't know,' she said.

'Still, your studies will continue for sure,' I said to prod her.

'Yes, then I can be anything!'

'Like...?' I asked.

'Teacher,' she replied after thinking about it for a while.

'Why teacher?' I asked.

Bhavna's answer wasn't merely an observation on the link between illiteracy and slavery; it captured an entire philosophy of life.

'I remember the day the circus pimp came to my house,' she said. 'He made my mother put her thumb impression on two blank sheets of paper because she could not read and write. That man brought us to India. After arriving here, we were abruptly awoken at 4 am the following day. The master there declared, "Come on, learn these tricks. Do your exercise." One or two masters would hold our feet and hands and twist our bodies in all directions. Before doing the exercise, a trainer asked us to change into the clothes provided by them. A woman handed us small knickers and vests which were visibly worn and dirty. We felt embarrassed and humiliated, and all of us girls burst into tears. Whenever we asked to be sent back to Nepal, the man from the circus would tell us that our parents had signed a ten-year agreement. No matter how many times we asked, that was the same response we always received... Because of my mother's illiteracy, I became a slave. I have been struggling since then. But I'm determined to learn to read and write once I'm back home. I will also teach others so they don't have to suffer like I did every day.'

An honest and poignant expression of the relationship between education and freedom such as this is rarely heard from even experienced educationists and social workers.

We sat there and ate together. Only after that did she feel confident enough to share with me all the things which I mentioned in the beginning. I spent the entire day there before heading home in the evening. It was immensely satisfying to witness Bhavna taking her first steps to reclaiming her lost childhood. She was brimming with happiness by the time I left. When we were about to leave, she came up to our car.

'Would you like to see a stunt?' she asked.

'Of course!' I said.

I got out of the car and stood there. In a flash, she jumped like a monkey and scrambled up the palm tree near the front. Then she leapt to another tree and hung from it with one hand. She got down from the tree, still laughing uproariously, and waved her other hand while shouting, 'Ta-ta, bye-bye!' But I called her to me to congratulate her. She clung to my chest and then dragged me to the gol kutiya, where Vishumala sat beaming.

In addition to the preparations to send the children back to Nepal, we were also trying to make arrangements for their education upon arrival, as well as to provide assistance to their parents. An organization from Hetauda had agreed to provide education and training to the girls in their residential school. An emotional farewell ceremony was held on the terrace of our office before sending them back. The children who had been freed, their parents, members of the Mukti Abhiyan Dal and office colleagues all joyfully covered each other with different colours, as if celebrating the festival of Holi. Everyone danced to the beats of the dholak while savouring the varied array of sweets.

The incident in Karnailganj sparked great awareness in India and Nepal, leading to boycotts of circuses in many cities of India and the release of some of the children held within them. The incident was widely publicized in Nepal's television and newspapers, impelling conscious citizens and youth to start chasing away traffickers coming from India. After some time, we filed a public interest litigation in the Supreme Court of India to ban child slavery from the entire circus industry, landmark orders for which were passed.

The Court directed the central government to issue a notification within two months to completely ban child labour in circuses. The honourable judges ordered the state governments to free children by raiding all the circuses together. The freed children were to be provided a safe place to stay in children's homes until they reached the age of eighteen. Officers of the central and state governments were expected to contact the parents of the rescued children, and if the parents wanted, they could take their children back home. The order demanded that the government plan and implement an effective rehabilitation programme for children rescued from circuses.

After almost five years, on 18 April 2011, the Court pronounced its full verdict. The judgment was historic in more ways than one, as it passed two very important orders. The first was related to trafficking, and the second to child labour. Before this case, the existing legal provisions were grossly inadequate in effectively addressing the issue of child labour and trafficking. The decision included provisions to clearly define all aspects of trafficking to prevent it. There was also an order for introducing urgent and comprehensive measures to eliminate child labour. It had far-reaching consequences. In light of that decision, a new law to stop child labour was passed, and a stricter legal provision to punish human trafficking was incorporated into the Indian Penal Code. A comprehensive law against trafficking is likely to be passed in the Parliament soon.

Bhavna had endured the anguish of dying every day and survived, and her life made possible the freedom of countless children in India. From what I know, after pursuing her studies for some time in Nepal, she got married. She now lives happily with her husband and mother, Vishumala. We also learnt that she had taken up a job. She may not have been able to fulfil her dream of becoming a teacher, but her children will never experience the hardships she faced in the absence of education.

The Fourteenth Cow in the Stable

This is the story of a plant in a green field, whose roots were infested with insects and stem fed with poison. This is the story of feet frozen in icy winter slush, hands carrying shovels heavier than their own weight, and a head burning with embers falling from the sky. This is the story of a child's heart that beat in rhythm with the hooves of cows and buffaloes. It is also a story of the child's helpless mother, stuck in the silence between two mutually unintelligible languages.

This is the story of Rakesh Sada, who was sold at a price less than that of the animals he lived with.

'Your Highness, my name is Rakesh Sada. I am from India, and I am here representing the countless children around the world who exist but are invisible. They have a voice but remain unheard. They have faces but have no identity.'

This was perhaps the first time that the Queen of Sweden had heard someone say such things. She kept looking at eleven-year-old Rakesh, speechless. This was in April 2007, when Rakesh Sada was in Stockholm, the capital of Sweden, for the World's Children's Prize for the Rights of the Child ceremony. The Queen, dressed in her regal attire, was presiding over the ceremony. Rakesh Sada wore his favourite white kurta-pyjama and jacket and sat royally beside the queen, with a bright smile. He was one of the jury members tasked with selecting the rightful recipient for the award, alongside other distinguished educationists, human rights activists and sociologists.

He takes great pride in his wisdom and intelligence in selecting the right person for the prize. Whenever he recounts the story of the jury's process, his face lights up with self-assurance, and an unmistakable gleam in his eyes.

'Look,' he says, 'the one I had chosen ultimately won the award. This means my selection was correct. I had picked the most deserving from among the contenders. That was Betty Makoni from Zimbabwe. Most of the jury members had come to the same decision.'

'But tell us, Rakesh ji, why exactly did you choose her?' I once joked with him. 'Maybe you found her more beautiful, or she flattered you with ice cream, chocolates, et cetera.'

'No, I chose Betty because she set up an organization for the welfare of numerous children, and is working hard for them. She herself used to work as a child labourer. She's committed to ensuring that children are granted their rights. She has saved the girls of three villages from different forms of abuse and exploitation, child labour, forced marriages, child trafficking and sexual abuse. She also established 500 girls' collectives in her own country. They have over 30,000 members. Following her example, other people have also begun to speak up for the rights of children. I had no choice but to choose her.'

Maybe for the same reason, Rakesh was invited once again to be part of the jury in 2008. Yet again, the woman whom Rakesh voted for eventually won the majority. This time it was Ms Somaly Mam, a child rights activist from Cambodia. She was combating the slavery of girls through her organization, Allyship, which operated three homes for the education and safety of the rescued girls.

The prize was founded in 2000 by Swedish child rights activists with the aim of promoting children's rights, democracy and friendship. They believed that at least two talented children should be included in the jury for the award. One of them should be a male or female student from Sweden, and the other a child advocating for children's rights in a developing nation. In 2006, the officials of the organization contacted us in their search for such a child. After considering all criteria, we chose Rakesh Sada and submitted his name to them, and they selected him.

By then, almost two years had passed since he had been living in Bal Ashram. He had achieved good grades in the third standard, and was now studying in the fourth at the village school. Rakesh was a cheerful, football-loving, intelligent and charming boy, always willing to lend a helping hand to his friends. He had interesting aspirations. For a few days he nurtured the dream of becoming a social worker and starting a movement against child labour. Then, when he scored a few goals in a football match, he would dream of becoming a renowned footballer. He was very fond of Kanhaiya Guruji. When Guruji taught him with love and tenderness, he became determined to take up teaching and impart knowledge to other children. However, if Guruji ever scolded him, he would stay away for days, set on becoming a policeman.

Rakesh was born in 1995, in the Ghina village in Saharsa district. This is a backward village with roughly six hundred houses, not unlike many other villages in Bihar. The section of the village with pucca houses made with bricks belonged to the Yadav community. A slender footpath from there leads to the Musahar Tola, where there are about eighty houses. In those days, the village had an old school with two classrooms, where students were taught up to the fifth grade.

'There were two pots of drinking water in the school,' he would tell us. 'One small, the other big. The small pot was new. The old pot was larger. The teachers used to send the children to fetch water from the well. Both teachers used to drink water from the small pot. The larger pot was meant for the children of the upper caste. Children from lower castes like us were not allowed to drink the water from either of them.'

Rakesh's father, Nunulal, had got him enrolled in school, but he was forced to drop out within a year due to two reasons. According to Rakesh, 'Children of the upper caste used to bring rugs from their homes to sit on, while we had to sit on the ground at the back. Our teachers used to twist their ears to punish them, but would beat us with a stick on our palms. There was a lot of discrimination.' The second reason for Rakesh to drop out of school was domestic. Nunulal had to work as an agricultural labourer on other people's farms because he had only about half an acre of land; despite the hard work his family put into it, there was not enough yield to sustain them. Nunu and his wife Teetiri had five children—three daughters and two sons. Rakesh was the youngest. The father had taken a loan of nine thousand rupees from a moneylender for the elder son Mukesh's marriage. Unable to repay the debt, he had decided to buy a goat with some of the money he had, and entrusted its care to Rakesh and his sister, Poonam. Rakesh often recounted his father's plan.

'He thought, "Let's get a goat; we can make some money off the milk and then sell the babies when they are grown. If they are males, they will bring us a profit when sold. If there are females, we can keep building our milk business by rearing them."'

Rakesh had had to drop out of school when he was five or six years old to carry through his father's plans. But Nunu's plan could not work. One evening, when both Rakesh and the goat did not return when they were supposed to, he broke down in tears. The goat was eventually found, but Rakesh remained missing. He checked with friends, family and scoured nearby areas, but there was no sign of him. Nunu did learn, however, that over the past two to three years, besides Rakesh, five more children had gone missing from neighbouring villages.

About four years after that, Nunu came to our Delhi office one day accompanied by his brother-in-law and an activist of Bachpan Bachao Andolan.

'Babuji,' he said, 'my wife and I are desperately trying to locate our son. We had to sell all our possessions, even our goat. Just recently, I found out something that could be of help. In the village nearby, there is a man named Ramchander Sada. He does not farm or do anything else for that matter. Yet he still manages to lead a luxurious life. He takes labourers to Punjab during the harvest season. He confirmed to me that he took Rakesh also.'

Nunu had gone to meet him, but he had refused to divulge

any information about Rakesh. After multiple visits to the man's house, Nunu ran into Ramchander's son one day. The boy, unaware of the situation, mentioned that his father had taken some children to Punjab too. Consequently, Nunu filed a complaint against Ramchander with the police for the abduction of his child.

'Did the policemen file your report so easily?' I asked.

'No,' he said, 'we pleaded and begged. They only registered the report when we bribed them with food and liquor. But they still didn't take any action. We went to the station many times in the following months and all but gave up in the end. We went to Ramchander's house too. We would cry and beg for help. Maybe that melted his wife's heart. She admonished her husband, saying that it was better to go hungry than to make money this way. Ultimately, on the condition that the police were not to be informed, Ramchander revealed that Rakesh had been taken to Punjab.'

Nunu kept his word and did not tell anyone about it. Subsequently, Ramchander told him that the boy was in the Jansa village of Amritsar district in Punjab. He and his son-in-law set off immediately for Jansa, which was about four or five kilometres from the city of Amritsar. They combed through the village for two days in search of their son. Though they didn't find Rakesh, they did discover that some children from Bihar were employed in the village. However, nobody could tell them exactly where those children worked. In the end, the two were forced to go back home without the boy.

I asked him why he didn't go to the police in Punjab.

'We were unfamiliar with the language and didn't have the money to bribe them with good food and liquor,' he replied. 'We were in a foreign land. Who would have listened to us? Rakesh's mother was furious and accused me of not trying hard enough to find our son. She asked me why I had come back from Punjab without Rakesh, and then insisted on going there to find him herself.'

'Did she go to Punjab, then?' I asked him.

'Yes, it took us almost a year to get everything ready,' he replied. 'I was already heavily in debt and it was a struggle to save enough for the journey. We could leave for Punjab only after we had collected enough money.'

Nunu continued, 'When we visited Punjab, we discovered that Rakesh was living in Sardar Sukhwinder Singh's two-story concrete mansion. Most of the dwellings in the village were quite sizable. We had not seen such grand houses ever. Seeing two tractors, a jeep and two motorcycles in the yard of the house, we concluded that the owner must be quite rich. This apprehension and fear kept us from knocking on their iron door. After we had been waiting outside for two to three hours, a man emerged from the house. We pleaded with him a long time, and he finally confirmed that a boy named Rakesh had worked there, but he didn't any longer because he had passed away a year ago. Teetiri and I lost our minds. We were in a state of shock and grief long after he left. Later, we took the bus to Amritsar and returned home by train.'

After reaching the village, they went straight to Ramchander. He told them that someone had seen Rakesh a few days ago, which meant that the man at Sukhwinder Singh's house had lied. Nunu went to the police station once again, and happened to run into a man whose son we had helped to free from a carpet factory in Uttar Pradesh. It was he who introduced Nunu to our colleague. Rakesh's parents had new hope for finding their son.

After learning the full story, I entrusted my senior colleague, Rakesh Sengar, with the mission of locating his namesake and liberating him. He first dispatched an activist, Sunny Singh, to Punjab accompanied by Nunu. Sunny, a Sikh youth whose mother tongue was Punjabi, was threatened and driven away by Sukhwinder and his men. They even let loose their ferocious pet dogs on our colleagues. They managed somehow to save their lives and get to the police station. Sukhwinder was a man of influence. After some time, he arrived at the police station himself. The sub-inspector and he threatened our people and asked them to leave the village immediately or face investigation for theft and dacoity. However, two key facts were revealed during the altercation. One, that Rakesh was still alive. Two, he was bought from Ramchander by Sukhwinder's father-in-law, Dilbagh Singh, for six thousand rupees (about 80 USD).

It took nearly two months to prepare for the rescue of Rakesh. During that time, the guardians of three other missing children had also come to us. Under the guidance of Sengar, our team took everyone along and journeyed to Amritsar. The superintendent of police, realizing the gravity of the situation, instructed the station house officer to take immediate action and rescue the children. Subsequently, Rakesh Sada and the three other children were rescued, while Sukhwinder was arrested by the police. Incidentally, Ramchander was in Punjab at the time and he too was nabbed.

Our colleagues returned to Delhi the following morning with the children and their parents. As soon as I heard the news, I came to the office. Teetiri was sitting on the sofa in the reception room, holding on tightly to her son. There was a cup of tea in the hand which cradled Rakesh, while with the other she kept wiping her tears of joy. I quietly sat down on the sofa next to her.

My attention was soon drawn to a heartbreaking little detail. Teetiri was desperately trying to communicate with her son. Rakesh too was trying to say something to his mother. I realized that they couldn't understand each other, since the mother spoke her rustic Maithili dialect, while the son spoke Punjabi. The mother did not know a single word of Punjabi, and Rakesh seemed to have completely forgotten his native language. Unfortunately, neither of them could speak Hindi fluently. As I sat there feeling miserable for not being able to understand either of the two languages, I could scarcely imagine the distress of both mother and child, unable to talk after a five-year-long separation.

We kept them in the office for a few days till we completed the legal formalities.

'Ramchander gave me a few sweets and tempted me with a lot more,' Rakesh told us one day. He spoke in his hybrid tongue. 'He then took me and five other children on a bus to Saharsa, where he treated us to sweets once again. We had a lot of fun and enjoyed the experience of travelling by train for the first time. We were on the train for two days and nights. On the third day, we got off at a station and then boarded a bus with Ramchander to yet another place. He had promised to take us home in the morning, but instead, he sold me to Dilbagh Singh for six thousand rupees. Later, he sold the rest of the children to other people for twelve thousand rupees. I was handed over to Sardar Sukhwinder Singh. He was a relative of Dilbagh Singh.

'In the beginning, I had to sweep his house, and in return, I would get the leftover rotis. Gradually, I was also made to clean cow and buffalo dung, bathe and wash them, and feed and give them water. I had to remain in the stable with the cows and buffaloes. For four years, I would sleep in a corner on a jute cloth. The most challenging part of the night was shielding myself from the cattle's dung and urine. There were fourteen of us in the stable. The cows, the buffaloes...and I was the fourteenth. Every night, Sardarji would lock the stable from the outside.'

Rakesh then recounted his daily routine. 'We servants had to get up at five in the morning to begin cleaning the stable. Not only the excrement of the animals, but also our own. Sometimes I was forced to urinate there during the night. Later, the house needed to be cleaned. Then, fodder and water had to be provided for the animals. I would often take a bath at the tubewell in the backyard. Roti was served with tea or buttermilk. One of the servants there, Bagga, was a very kind person. He would often come over from the adjacent hall and put his blanket over me. As a Sikh, he was allowed to visit the gurudwara on festivals and would save me some of the halwa and poori he got there. He was the only one who looked like he cared for us... When I grew up, I had to work in the fields.'

By 'grew up', he meant that he reached the age of eight/nine. He was ten years old now. He had an innocent face but hands and feet hard as stone.

'Many a time,' he went on, 'we were woken up at three or four o'clock in the night and sent along with a servant to water the fields. As the power was cut from six in the morning, it was essential to do the watering before that. Sometimes, due to the rapid flow of water, the earthen ramparts in the fields would break, and along with the other labourers, I would have to lie down at the breach to prevent the water from flowing out.'

'Did you need to do the same thing even in winters?' I asked him.

He said that he did. 'Whatever the season, be it summer, winter, rain, we had to do the same thing. In Bihar, only one crop was grown in the whole year, but in Punjab there were three to four crops in a year. One thing was different during the winters though. Sardarji would add a pill to the tea before sending us to the field. After drinking the tea, we did not feel any trace of cold at all. He would also give us two to four spoons of alcohol in water at night.'

In order to make agricultural labourers work even in the coldest weather conditions, opium is sometimes mixed in their tea. Even as their hands become swollen from irrigating the fields in winter, the opium numbs the pain. According to official statistics, fifty lakh (five million) children—with unofficial estimates ranging from five to six crores (fifty to sixty million)—are engaged in child labour in our country. Approximately two-thirds of them are engaged in agricultural work. There is no legal prohibition on employing children in the fields. In most countries, including the United States, child labour is not banned in agriculture. But farming was not as hazardous thirty to forty years ago as it is now. Toxic pesticides, chemical fertilizers, electricity, tractors, etc., are commonly used in farming now. The use of machines in all operations like sowing, reaping, weeding and threshing has become the usual practice.

While living in our office, Rakesh mixed really well with everyone, and the staff would often joke about his unique mix of Maithili, Punjabi and Hindi. We got him and his parents new clothes. One day, he walked into my room donning a brand-new pair of pants, shirt and shoes. He had got a pair of dark sunglasses with a colleague's help, and now stood before me wearing them with a broad smile.

'How do I look, sir?' he asked.

To which I replied in Punjabi, '*Vadda sohna lag riya si, puttar* (You look smashing, son).'

It was all that was required to make Rakesh laugh out loud. He came behind my chair and started shaking me by my shoulders. He mumbled in a mischievous tone, asking me why I didn't talk to him in Punjabi all these days if I knew the language. I explained to him that I could not speak more than two or three sentences in Punjabi.

Rakesh was jubilant that day, having donned new clothes for

the first time in what felt like ages. He had been a small child when he was taken away and couldn't recall much from his time at home. By the simple act of wearing new clothes he had found a new sense of confidence, inspiring within him the desire to go back to school. Indeed he had come to tell me that he wanted to go to school on the pretext of showing me his new clothes. I was overjoyed and assured him that after speaking to his parents, he would be called to Bal Ashram, where he would be able to learn and read as much as he wished.

I asked him what he wanted to be when he grew up.

After a moment of thought, he replied, 'I want to own buffaloes so I can consume their milk myself. I'll build a room above the stables for the caretakers to stay in.'

I was simply delighted by that little boy's response. I embraced and kissed him. The family happily went back to their village a few days later.

In early 2006, Rakesh came to Bal Ashram, where he spent about six months in preparation before he was admitted to grade three at the local government school. For the first year or two, he struggled to concentrate on his studies. Due to his addiction to opium and alcohol at an early age, he likely found it hard to focus on anything, among other issues. His food intake was also very low. He displayed baffling temperamental contradictions. On the one hand, he was a very lazy and pessimistic child; on the other, he was eager to study and learn. His eyes betrayed the lack of trust he had in himself and in others. He often lied. He would resort to lies to cover up his mistakes. But he was an astute observer of other people.

Kanhaiya Guruji, Rakesh's favourite teacher, not only taught the children dance and art, but also trained them in meditation, yoga, exercise and drama. Rakesh's enthusiasm soon led him to take an avid interest in drama and painting. In our play, *Bachche*

Kahan Gaye? ('Where Have the Children Gone?'), he began with playing a goat, but soon took up the roles of the shepherd boy and teacher. On the festival of Dussehra, he would make the audience laugh uproariously with his portrayal of a comical demon in the Ramleela play.

For many years, the role of Ravana was played by a child named Vijay. We used to say at the Ashram that if the actual Ravana were to appear, he would be confused which of them was the real demon. Vijay is now a thirty-year-old family man. He used to be a talented actor, and was a great friend of Rakesh when he was living at the Ashram. There were a couple of other reasons that led to their friendship of course, besides playing demons in the Ramleela. Vijay, like Rakesh, spent his early years in a village where he worked in the fields. So they were both interested in gardening as well. And they were very talkative, these two, often chatting for hours. Like his friend, Vijay too had initially been a slacker, but had grown out of it.

Bal Ashram's blooming flowers, plants and lush grass owe much to the efforts of Vijay apart from those of Sumedha ji. Hailing from the Supaul district in Bihar, which borders Nepal, he was forced to work in the sugarcane fields at the tender age of ten. He was incredibly articulate and well spoken, and so his sugarcane field owners began to use him for other purposes. They covertly sent him to transport insecticides, chemical fertilizers and cough medicines to Sunsari and Saptari districts in Nepal, and to bring back some goods in return. He believes that these goods contained illicit drugs, which he used to transport on a bicycle.

In 2002, the activists of Bachpan Bachao Andolan rescued Vijay from his exploitative owners and brought him to Bal Ashram. His amiable nature led to him becoming good friends with all the other children. He was a helpful child and pretty soon came to excel in his studies too. During summer visits to his village, he would work towards getting the children there out of labour and enrolling them in schools. In 2005, he was felicitated by the Bharat Scouts and Guides at the Rajasthan state level for liberating hundreds of children from child labour. Upon completion of his higher secondary education, he joined the Mukti Caravan full-time. He had spent all his earnings on the medical treatment of his ailing father, who unfortunately did not survive. After his death, Vijay raised and educated both his younger brothers. He now lives in Bal Ashram where his main responsibility is to oversee work related to government departments concerning children. He has acquired a master's in Social Work and his wife too has completed her master's degree. They have two children, a son and a daughter.

'Rakesh was very fond of sleeping,' says Kanhaiya Guruji, both Vijay and Rakesh's favourite teacher. 'Depending on the season, the daily routine of children started with waking up at five or six in the morning. He used to retreat to a corner and doze off. But I knew how to deal with him. To wake him up in the summer, I would splash water on his face, which would leave him grumpy for a few hours. Then, whenever he found an opportunity, he would say his favourite line, "Sorry, Guruji, sorry," and start smiling.'

With the efforts of Kanhaiya, Ramkripal Guruji and others, Rakesh's conduct began to improve. He took interest in both studying and playing a variety of sports. He returned from his first trip to Sweden with such enthusiasm and joy that he could barely find the words to speak about it. But he seemed to have become an expert in shaking hands and hugging people! As soon as he came back to Bal Ashram, he began offering handshakes to every single person he ran into. Then he proceeded to hug and kiss all of them. The children and teachers had tremendous fun teasing him.

Sometimes at the Ashram, we have competitions of eating and drinking, to see who can consume the most fruits, sweets, laddoos or sherbet, for the entertainment of children. On one occasion, a banana-eating competition was held. We had estimated that around eighty children would be able to consume up to seven hundred bananas. And we bought big ones too. But they proved to be too few. We had to dispatch cars three times during the competition to purchase bananas from the market. Our children devoured around 1,600 bananas that day! Rakesh Sada won the competition by eating twenty-four bananas, then thirty-two pooris, and finally thirty-eight laddoos, thereby earning the title of 'Greatest Glutton' in the Ashram.

Rakesh was enjoying himself here, playing sports and studying hard. But he had to leave the Ashram in December 2009 to go back home. His father had taken out a loan of sixteen thousand rupees for his daughter's marriage. Additionally, he had also spent the entire amount received for the rehabilitation of his son under the government scheme. Teetiri had been suffering from an illness for several months and would often call Rakesh on the phone to express her sorrow. Eventually, Rakesh returned to his village, but we made sure through our friends there that he joined the fifth grade in a local school.

The issues of children going missing, child trafficking, bonded labour and agricultural child labour all overlap in Rakesh's distressing story. But his story is also one of freedom, dreams, possibilities, accomplishments and justice. Rakesh recognizes this fact. I received a call from him one day. He was still in his village at the time, studying in the eighth grade. He sounded a bit too enthusiastic. After discussing some unimportant matters, he came to the point.

'Almost three hundred students come to study at my school in Dakiya. Most of them are girls. Do you know, Bhai Sahab ji, how this has come about?'

'Your village must have many girls,' I said, pulling his leg. 'Maybe twice as many as the boys. That's why there are more of them in the school.'

'No, no,' he replied. 'Don't you have faith in my abilities? Everyone here knows my story. They've seen my pictures with the Queen of Sweden that were published in the local newspapers. Over the last year, I have been visiting people's homes to emphasize the importance of educating girls. Maybe that's why it wasn't too hard to get so many girls accepted into the school. No child-trafficking pimps can even enter the villages of Padampur, Ghina and Dakiya!'

Sometimes, for fun, I used to joke with him that he should get educated so that later he could take a loan from the bank and open a stable of buffaloes. To this he responded that his aspirations had changed and he now wanted to become an activist of Bachpan Bachao Andolan.

But life is not a straight line, which one can draw to connect one point to another, nor is it a predictable curve whose turns can be seen coming. Perhaps it is like wet soil or like a flowing river. Rakesh strove to overcome difficult circumstances, but was often forced to accept defeat. He was always burdened with issues concerning his family. In 2011, he went to Haryana with a group of teenagers from his village to earn some money. He laboured as a porter in the vegetable market. Returning to the village after about six months, he called me and told me that he had saved twelve thousand rupees (about 150 USD) from his wages and handed them over to his father. It had helped Nunu repay the entire loan taken for his daughter's marriage.

'I will never return to that market,' he told me. 'I had to stay up all night unloading vegetables from the trucks. I had to wash and store rotten fruits and vegetables. I would witness the owners wrapping up and selling poisonous spices by packaging them well. I definitely do not want to make money through dishonest means. Absolutely not. Sometimes I thought that there would be violence and bloodshed in the mandi. I'm now nearly seventeen years old, but I saw a number of younger children working in abhorrent conditions in the marketplace. How could I bear to see this? I remained silent though. I had to earn money to pay off my father's debt. But now I will return there as an activist and free those children.'

Rakesh came to Delhi after some time with the intention of liberating the enslaved child labourers as he had promised. Accompanied by one of our veteran colleagues, he journeyed to Panipat, to its bustling market which was too vast to conduct raids. However, Rakesh was aware of where the owner kept the children at night. So, in the middle of the night, about twenty Bihari children were rescued and eventually sent back to their villages. But instead of going back home after this, Rakesh took up a job in another town in Haryana. There, he managed to earn and save about fifteen thousand rupees (about 200 USD) in four months, with which he returned to his village and opened a small shop of eateries.

Rakesh used to serve Indian-style burgers at his food stall, earning three to four hundred rupees a day, enough to sustain a family in the village. He wanted to expand his business gradually. He had strategically placed his shop at an ideal location, so he could keep a watchful eye over the paths leading to and from neighbouring villages, to prevent traffickers from kidnapping children. He consistently reported his findings to the offices of Bachpan Bachao Andolan in Bihar and Delhi. During that time, he even got married and, within a few years, had become the father of two sons.

All seemed to be going well but his life took another drastic turn when the land on which his food stall stood was expropriated for road construction, forcing him to close it.

In 2020, Rakesh Sada celebrated his twenty-fifth birthday. Currently, he is employed in a rice mill in Haryana. After saving sufficient funds, he hopes to return to his village and start a new business there. But no matter where he resides or how he earns a living, I am sure he will always continue his work to combat child labour and illiteracy.

'Please Save Me, Bhaiya Ji'

This is a story of a spark, a torch, of heat and light. It is also a story of birds, gazing at you and me through the bars of the cage they're in, of their restless wings, and of the cool breeze and the open sky which they long for. It is also a story of the earth, of moulded clay, of red bricks made with the blood and sweat of children, of towering buildings, and of the civilized people who live within them.

Born as slaves in the largest democracy of the world, this is the story of Sabo and Gulabo, and the first steps of the movement against modern slavery. Here is also the start of my own journey. It tells the tale of the death of God's most beautiful creation, in my arms. It is about the numerous sparks of freedom that it ignited.

This is the story of two of my girls who I got to spend very little time with. They were with me for a total of three days each. And yet, both of them had a profound influence on my life. Their pain served as the catalyst for our movement against modern slavery.

We rescued fifteen-year-old Sabo in March 1981, and fourteen-year-old Gulabo in August 1983. For the first few years, Sabo would visit me, but then she moved to her in-laws' home after her marriage. We were never in regular touch after that. As for Gulabo, she cannot visit me any more. She took her last breath with her head on my lap.

Both of them had worked as labourers at brick kilns.

Let me first talk about my last meeting with Sabo. It was some day in May 1985. I was sitting in my office in Jantar Mantar, New Delhi, working in the afternoon as usual. All of a sudden, accompanied by her groom, Sabo rushed into my room looking resplendent in a sparkling new salwar-kameez and adorned with jewellery.

'Bhaiya ji! Can you guess who this is?' she exclaimed as she gave me a big hug.

I playfully slapped her cheek, and said with a mischievous smile, 'No. Is this the one you ran away with?'

She paused for a second and, scrunching her nose and lips, retorted, 'What do you mean? I already introduced him to you and you liked him too. Are you pulling my leg?'

I rose from my chair, laughing heartily, and embraced Sabo and her groom warmly. Sumedha ji and I had, unfortunately, been unable to attend her wedding. But we were sure that she would visit us soon.

'We have to leave for Ajmer Sharif immediately,' she said. 'Your blessings are always with me, but this time I have come to get *him* your blessings. I decided we'll go to pray at Khwaja Sahib's dargah only after that.'

'Do you think I'll let Mr Groom go just like that? Come and sit!' I said. I was overwhelmed by her love and respect for me.

There was a shop in front of our office that served South Indian food. I quickly sent someone to get something for them. We used to have a credit account at that shop, so there was no payment to worry about just now. I was more concerned about something else. My younger sister and brother-in-law had come to visit me for the first time after marriage, and I would have to send them off without a gift. I somehow collected a little money from my colleagues and made arrangements for it.

This had happened for the second time. A few months after Sabo and her family had been freed, it was Raksha Bandhan. Sumedha ji had taken our son to her maternal home in Karol Bagh. I was on my way to the office when I suddenly began missing my elder sister, who lives in my hometown, Vidisha. To my amazement, when I arrived at the office, I discovered that my younger sister was already there, waiting. I hadn't expected to see Sabo today; she had even brought along her father, Wasal Khan. Except for a handful of people, Raksha Bandhan is not widely celebrated among Muslim families. Sabo tied the rakhi on my wrist with immense affection. And I had no gift to give her, even money. Fortunately, Sumedha ji came to the office in the evening and gave Sabo a gift. This little tradition of ours was observed for many years that followed. In the beginning, she used to come to tie the rakhi herself, then she started sending her rakhis by post.

It had been nearly a year since they had been freed from the kiln when I received a letter from Sabo. In the letter, she bemoaned her father's plans to wed her to an older man who was already married. We sent a colleague to bring Wasal Khan to Delhi. I explained his mistake to him while also admonishing him severely for it. He acknowledged his fault and called off the wedding. Approximately eighteen months later, Wasal returned to us with some of his family members. Among them was a young man of about twenty. Wasal told us that Sabo had agreed to an arranged marriage with him, and he wanted my opinion on it. He seemed like a good lad and I supported their decision. Sabo was soon married to that boy.

As I said my goodbyes to Sabo and her husband that May afternoon in 1985, I jokingly said, 'Ask for a couple of blessings for me too when you offer a chadar at the dargah sharif.'

She smiled and replied, 'Yes, I'll definitely do that.'

'What will you ask for?' I asked her.

'I will ask that you become a lawyer,' she said.

I laughed and said, 'But I don't want to become a lawyer.'

To this, she said, without missing a beat, 'Then I will pray that Sona Bhaiya [my son, Bhuwan] grows up to be a lawyer soon.'

Lawyers had, in fact, played a major role in securing Sabo's freedom. She would frequently hear her father mention the term 'Vakil Sahib', and so she believed that lawyers were the most powerful and helpful people there were.

'Would you pray for me to become the uncle of a lovely niece?' I asked Sabo.

'Of course,' she said softly, blushing a little, 'I will pray for a lovely daughter for you too.'

I kept thinking about Sabo for a long time after she left. My mind went back to the first time I met Wasal Khan.

It was the year 1981. Along with some of my friends, I used to publish a magazine titled *Sangharsh Jaari Rahega* ('The Struggle

Will Live On'). The fortnightly magazine was dedicated to highlighting the issues of the most disadvantaged and oppressed groups in our country. One day, I was sitting in my office when a distressed man suddenly knocked on my door. He was Sabo's father, Wasal Khan. Someone had told him that we could publish his story in our magazine, which might be of some help to him. What Wasal Khan proceeded to tell me left me shocked and enraged. Seventeen years ago, a dealer had lured him and his newly married wife from his village in Aligarh to work in a brick kiln. He had taken many people there in the same manner. That kiln was near the city of Sirhind in Punjab. All of them had worked there as slaves ever since. They were not permitted to leave the kiln compound. Provided with the basic necessities, they were not even paid any wages.

Sabo was born at the kiln fourteen years ago. One day, Wasal learnt that some pimps from a Delhi brothel had come to purchase her. They were inside one of the rooms making a deal by groping Sabo's body to decide on a price for her. The deal could not be sealed that day because the kiln owner demanded more than the buyers were willing to pay. Wasal fled to Chandigarh in a truck in the dead of night, hoping to find some assistance. He stumbled upon a man who was a subscriber of our magazine, which eventually led him to me. He fell at my feet as he wept recounting his tale.

I was twenty-seven years old at the time. A thought crossed my mind: What if Sabo was my daughter or sister? Would I have squandered a whole day to merely write her story? When I informed Wasal that I was going to Sirhind to rescue Sabo and his family instead of publishing his story, he panicked.

'The owners are very dangerous and powerful. They'll kill you if you go there!' he exclaimed.

I somehow convinced him and took him home. We had

rented a small storeroom in someone's house, where Sumedha ji and I lived with our one-and-a-half-year-old son, Bhuwan. I told Wasal I needed to make some arrangements and reassured him that we would go to free Sabo in two or three days.

After a few days of careful planning and preparation, my colleague Jaisingh from Punjab and I, along with some other friends, travelled to the kiln in Sirhind. We had hired a truck to transport the families of the kiln workers with us. It so happened that there was only one watchman there at the time whom we managed to drive away. Sabo ran to her father and embraced him when she saw him enter the boundary wall with the rest of us. That was the first time I saw her. Wasal Khan convinced the workers to come with us, and within a few minutes, all the children, women and men had boarded the truck. There were thirty-six individuals in all.

Just as we were about to depart, the owner of the property arrived in a jeep accompanied by his armed guards and police officers, thus confirming Wasal's fears. The workers were forcefully pulled out of the truck and shoved back towards the kiln. Wasal Khan was apprehended and viciously beaten, and so were we. We only managed to save our lives by sprinting through the fields, eventually making our way back to Chandigarh and then to Delhi. One of my friends had taken many pictures there with his camera, providing us with good evidence. With the help of a lawyer friend, we knocked on the doors of the High Court in Delhi and our request was heard. Within days, the court passed a direction for the release of all thirty-six people, including Sabo. To my knowledge, this was the first instance of the emancipation of slaves through civic action in modern times.

As I took the freed children from the court to my office that day, I experienced what it meant to be free. In that moment, I clearly saw my life's purpose. The children joyfully bounced around on the broad roads of Delhi, a city of towering buildings and busy roads with shiny cars, something they had never seen in their lives. As I looked at them, I felt like I was the one being liberated. The traffic jam built up, but these children didn't have a care in world and refused to even hold their parents' hands.

We reached our office. First, we took everyone to the canteen on the ground floor of the building. They had to be convinced to use the chairs to sit down. We had invited a few journalists, and this too was a new experience for them. With cameras, pens and notebooks in hand, they began to collect as much information as they could. One of the journalists placed a cup of tea in front of Sabo, but she refused to touch it as she had never tasted tea before. Assuming that she had refused because she was a child, the man had a glass of milk brought for her instead. Sabo shyly withdrew at the sight of the cup of milk. There were no milch animals at the kiln where she worked. She had never had milk after her mother had stopped breastfeeding her as a toddler. Out of curiosity, a journalist showed her some coins.

'The contractor wouldn't even let us play with bricks and pieces of coal. These toys are so shiny!' she exclaimed, taking them in her hand.

The girl who was being traded for thousands of rupees did not know what coins were. Her skin had been scorched black by fires in the kiln, but she had never had a cup of tea or warm milk.

From the Indus Valley civilization to present times, bricks have been a hallmark of modernity and prosperity. This essential building material is used across the world in a variety of construction work. As for its manufacture, in India, estimates suggest that approximately ten million labourers are employed in about 150,000 brick kilns across the country. Furthermore, it is believed that up to twenty-five to thirty million tonnes of coal are burned in their production annually. There are three main categories of labourers that work in these kilns. First, the *pathers*, or stone workers, knead clay into a pulp which is then placed in moulds made of tin or wood. After the wet bricks have been left to dry in the moulds for some time, they carefully remove each brick and arrange them in neat rows, ensuring that none are crooked or broken. These bricks are then left out in the sun for a couple of days to dry completely.

The second category of labourers is that of the *jalaiwala*, who keeps the kiln burning. I still remember what a jalaiwala had once said to me, venting his pain and anger to a sympathetic listener.

'Sahib,' he remarked, 'the red bricks that you buy gain their colour not from the owner's coal, but from our blood.'

The third category is the *nikasiwala*, who removes the freshly-baked hot brick from the furnace.

The work of making bricks is not carried out during the rainy season. Labourers at many kilns leave for their villages when the monsoons arrive. But many of them are not granted permission to leave because it is not an easy task for the owners to find reliable craftsmen. To make up for this, they give them loans through the traffickers, a system that effectively ensnares them in a cycle of debt.

I had once visited the villages of Singhbhum district with my friend, Laro Jonko, who is a Ho tribal woman and activist, in an effort to free the kiln workers there. We encountered numerous girls, young and old women who were completely bald. This was very unusual for the people of this region.

On inquiry, we discovered that the job of these women was to haul the finished product from the kiln. They had lost all their hair from carrying the burden of hot bricks on their heads all day. But the primary concern of their families was that nobody would marry their bald daughters. We also came across a number of girls who were pregnant as a result of sexual assault by the kiln owners. Some of the young girls had been forced to have abortions. Many of the women had been lured from impoverished regions of West Bengal to the kilns with the simple promise of a new sari or blouse. Once here, they were subjected to sexual abuse on a regular basis. The tribal girls that worked there were used to not wearing undergarments before coming to the kiln. To them, the kiln owner and his accomplices would offer brightly-coloured blouses and underpants, bringing them over as bonded labourers and exploiting them sexually. Over the past forty years, our organization has managed to free hundreds of such girls who have survived sexual exploitation.

We provided a temporary safe space to stay for the people rescued from Sirhind in an open field in front of our office. With the assistance of our friends and acquaintances we managed to procure food and water for them, but it took an additional two days to collect the funds needed to send them back to their respective villages. Wasal Khan and the other adults were desperate to return. The children, however, had only ever known the kiln and never been to a village before. They were celebrating their newfound freedom.

Sabo was an incredibly chatty and rather innocent girl. In the three days that she spent with us, she became close with my family. Our son was like a toy for her. He was a handsome, cuddly and friendly child, and Sabo never wanted to put him down. She would tease me.

'Bhaiya ji,' she would say, 'this doesn't look like your son! He looks just like my beautiful Bhabhi.' Then, she would whisper in my ear, 'I was just joking. He has your face. He smiles like you too. But yes, the fair complexion has definitely been inherited from his mother.'

When it was time for them to go, a colleague of mine and I

rented a truck to take them to the newly constructed Interstate Bus Stand of Delhi (ISBT). I had never been there before, and I was amazed to see the dozens of stands, arranged in a pattern that looked like a maze to me. I made them sit in a corner and went to find the Aligarh bus stand. When I returned, Sabo and two other children were missing. The worried parents of the children told me that they had followed me. After a frantic search of ten to fifteen minutes, we finally found them among a crowd of onlookers watching a dancing bear. They were laughing, clapping and jumping with joy.

The bus arrived in a few minutes, and the passengers jostled one another to get on board. Some of them had tears streaming down their faces. Wasal Khan and his wife hugged me tightly, both of them crying. Sabo didn't come to me. I wasn't surprised though. She was sitting on the back seat with her tattered scarf covering her face. She was sobbing as I approached her. She grasped my hand and put her face on it, her tears soaking my palm. I broke down too. Suddenly, she rose from her seat and began to plead with me.

'Bhaiya ji, take me back with you. I want to stay with you and Bhabhi ji.'

After much convincing and a promise to see her again soon, she finally took her seat. The bus eventually took off.

Wasal Khan used to visit us from time to time, often bringing information about people from nearby villages who were being held captive somewhere. Sabo would tag along with him to come and meet us sometimes. She never came after her visit to Ajmer Sharif, but I was sure she prayed for us. Perhaps her prayers had been accepted. After a few years, on the day of Raksha Bandhan, our daughter Asmita was born. She has been active in fighting for child rights since her childhood. Our son, Sona, aka Bhuwan, is today one of the foremost human rights lawyers in the country fighting against child slavery, bonded labour, human trafficking and other issues.

One reason why we lost contact with Sabo is that we had to frequently change offices due to the attacks that we faced. Unfortunately, many of the documents, including the records of addresses, were looted or destroyed in such incidents. And so, it became that much more difficult to find Wasal Khan or Sabo.

The liberation of Sabo motivated me to start the Bachpan Bachao Andolan and several other national and international initiatives and campaigns. It was, however, the sacrifice of Gulabo which helped transform the initial spark ignited by Sabo into a blazing torch.

In August 1983, we received reports of some families being held captive as bonded labourers at a brick kiln in Mahendragarh district, in the state of Haryana. We filed a public interest litigation in the Supreme Court of India for their release. The Court, accepting the case, appointed Ghanshyam Pardeshi, an independent journalist, as the commissioner to take action on the issue. I went out one night with Pardeshi ji to look for the bonded labourers. Suddenly, we found ourselves caught in a fierce storm. The strong winds and heavy rain made it incredibly difficult for me to handle the vehicle. Finding the village and the kiln was no easy task even without it. But Pardeshi ji was a jovial man. He was from Assam and spoke Hindi with an amusing Assamese accent. He kept teasing me and singing a Hindi film song loudly in his thick accent: '*Borka rani, jora jor se borso.*' (Oh, queen of rain, come down forcefully.) He was basically trying to lighten the mood.

The owner of the kiln had sent the labourers away to a different location prior to our arrival. We had taken two policemen with us from the police station, which was approximately thirty kilometres away. Although we suspected that the police or the government's lawyer had already warned the kiln owner about us, we went to multiple kilns in the area, searching for the families despite the rain with the help of the jeep's headlights. The initial excursion, however, proved unsuccessful.

Instead of waiting until the morning, though, we began searching again even though it was past eleven in the night. We eventually learned from someone that, earlier in the evening, some people had been loaded into a truck and taken towards Rajasthan. Without delay, we sped in the direction of Rajasthan. We had travelled about twenty to twenty-five kilometres when we noticed some activity behind a thicket, in the shadows beside an unpaved road. When we pulled over, we saw that children, women and men were lying trembling in the dirt. They seemed disoriented and feeble. A few of them were sitting, tightly holding on to each other. A little girl lay next to them on a tattered old mattress, some among them attempting to shield her from the rain. The thin and sickly girl was Gulabo.

They were already extremely scared, and they became even more afraid to see us. We were able to calm them down, but getting them to a secure shelter was critical. Finding transportation in the dead of night was a difficult task. Pardeshi ji commanded the policemen to get hold of a truck or tractor trolley at all costs. I accompanied them as they set off towards the nearest town. As we reached a crossroads, we saw a few dhabas in the vicinity. Some trucks had been stalled on their journey due to the rain. We hired an empty truck to take us to Delhi. It was an open truck, but fortunately the rain was showing signs of slowing down.

We arrived in Delhi around five or six in the morning with forty-two people in tow. Our office was now in the South Avenue area of Delhi, which is the official residential area for members of parliament. An MP friend of ours had kindly lent us his plot. The forty-two people stayed there. We were especially concerned about Gulabo. The clothes that she and the others were wearing were nearly dry from the journey in the open truck, but she was still shaking and shivering. A thick carpet was spread on the floor of the large office room and she was taken there and made to sit on it. I then immediately took down some curtains from the windows with the help of a colleague and covered her with them. We had milk in our kitchen, so I quickly prepared two cups of strong tea and gave it to the girl as her mother applied some Vicks ointment to her body. I was extremely glad to see Gulabo smile as she sipped on the tea I had made. It felt even better when she said, 'Bhaiya ji, the tea is very good. I've never had tea like this before.'

Gulabo was fourteen years old, but looked much younger and thinner than her eight-year-old brother. She had been unwell for a few days, and there was no access to medicine at the kiln. Her fever and cough had worsened during the night, so I gave her a dose of paracetamol for her fever. But we still needed a doctor to come and see her. After a while, she got up and sat against the wall, looking around the room in astonishment.

'Bapu, where are we?' she asked Sube Singh, her father.

'I don't know where we are,' Sube replied, then added, pointing towards me, 'This Babuji has rescued us from the kiln and brought us here.'

Gulabo kept looking at me.

I sat down and stroked her head and said, 'Gulabo, you are in Delhi now. Now you are all free.'

She was still staring at me. Maybe she didn't understand me, or maybe she didn't trust me. Slowly, a few of the others began to gather around us. I reassured them that we were making preparations to take them back to their villages soon and that they had nothing to fear. I also assured them that their loans did not have to be repaid, and that, upon their return, they would be free to pursue whatever work they desired.

A warm smile spread across everyone's faces as soon as they heard this. My hand was still placed on Gulabo's head. Her hand reached out of the curtains and she excitedly said to her mother, 'Can we really go home? Let's go quickly!'

Soon after, I noticed many of the women and men tying up their bundles. I explained to them that they should rest for the time being, as it would be about noon by the time they could head back to their villages. So they opened the bundles and put their clothes out to dry in the open field in front of the office. I too stepped out with them, to soak in the joy of liberation that could be seen glowing on their faces.

They could not be sent to the village that day because the statements of Ghanshyam Pardeshi and others had not been recorded. Gulabo's health was better now. She had eaten some bread with tea. On the advice of a friend who was a doctor, I had given her some medicines for fever and cough. We had scheduled an appointment for the following day to take her for a proper check-up.

Her temperature had not risen since the morning on the second day. However, in the afternoon, she developed high fever accompanied by shivering. When I received a call from her father, Sube Singh, I arrived to find her thrashing her hands and feet about. She was babbling incoherently, calling out for her parents. Her mother was crying, desperately pleading for help, 'Babuji, please save my daughter!' Sube Singh stood behind, silent tears streaming down his face as he stared at me. I sat there and gently stroked Gulabo's head, her body racked with high fever. We applied cold water compresses to her head right away and eventually her fever began to subside. I instructed one of my employees to make the necessary arrangements to get her to the hospital quickly.

It had been several hours since Gulabo had been laying in her mother's lap. I tenderly lifted her head and cradled it on mine. Between coughs, she opened her eyes and pleaded.

'I don't want to die. Please save me.'

She looked at me, her eyes filled with hope for some kind of a miracle. She was in unbearable pain. She held on to me tightly with one hand and her mother with the other. Slowly, her grip began to weaken. Her eyes suddenly widened and a desperate plea escaped her lips as she took in two or three shuddering breaths.

'Save me, Bhaiya ji. Save me, Amma!'

Those were her last words. She passed away in my arms. I was unable to take in what had just happened. I could not have imagined that she would die. We kept calling out to her while desperately massaging her hands and feet, but there was no response from her.

I frantically grabbed Gulabo and ran outside to my jeep, with Sube Singh in tow. We drove straight to Ram Manohar Lohia Hospital, one of the most renowned government hospitals in Delhi. My heart raced as I fervently prayed for divine intervention. Maybe she would open her eyes again. The doctors announced her dead on arrival when we reached the Emergency room. She would need to be taken for a post-mortem examination, we were told. Sube Singh was handed over Gulabo's body by the afternoon on the following day, after many disconsolate hours of running around in the heat. Her post-mortem report indicated that her death was caused by tuberculosis, which had completely destroyed both her lungs. Additionally, she suffered from severe malnutrition.

The hospital staff asked Sube Singh to sign some papers. His response summed up in one sentence his helplessness and the suffering he had lived through over many years past.

'Doctor Sahib,' he said, 'if I could read and write, my daughter would not have died such an undignified death.'

They accepted his thumb impression with my signature. Sube and I took Gulabo's lifeless body in our jeep to the electric crematorium near Nigambodh Ghat. After completing the necessary procedures, I placed the body in the tray. Sube, standing next to me, was sobbing uncontrollably. Perhaps I had never seen a more helpless and miserable man in my life. This unfortunate father could not even carry his daughter to the hospital, and now from the hospital to the crematorium, in his own arms. He had lost his right hand many years ago. An accident at the kiln had left his hand severely burned. And due to lack of adequate medical care, he had had to undergo an amputation from the shoulder. As for his left hand, it too had suffered an injury in the commotion of the past two days.

Holding Sube's injured left hand with my own, I pushed the tray with Gulabo's body into the electric furnace. Standing in front of the blazing fire, he muttered with a cold sigh, 'Babuji, my daughter was already burnt to death. We are just burning her ashes again.' He was speaking the truth—a harsh, unequivocal truth. I can still hear Gulabo's desperate plea, 'Save me, Bhaiya ji!' ringing in my ears and fuelling my outrage and also my compassion.

I was fighting for freedom and justice for all bonded labourers, including children, until Gulabo's passing. After that tragedy, I shifted my entire focus to eradicating child slavery.

There Was Once a Girl Named Sultana

Birds, like the wind or the light, are not bound by borders, be they boundaries created by religion, or nations. This is the story of two free birds, one from Nepal and the other from Bangladesh, who had been forced by circumstance to be confined to the dark, obscure alleys they knew to be home.

But no matter how narrow, dingy, winding and uneven the streets may be, they are teeming with life. Though cloaked in darkness, they offer refuge to countless individuals—to weep freely and sleep soundly. This is a story of the fire that simmers within these streets, a fire that can melt hearts. It is the story of eyes and ears that search for love in every face and in every spoken word, even as a sea of love brims within them.

This is the story of Basu and Sultana, of aspirations that reach for the stars, with battered wings and a tenacity that never falters.

It was 14 January 1998. We were in the midst of the preparations for the Global March Against Child Labour in Manila. We had started this march to mobilize a global movement against child labour, to advocate for an international law to bring an end to such exploitation of children. Apart from Manila, the march was to commence from two other places as well—Cape Town and Sao Paulo.

I was sitting with the fifty or so children who had also arrived in Manila to join the march. They had come from about twenty countries across the world. As we were chatting, my eyes fell on the youngest child there. His eyes reflected confidence and curiosity, but also a deep desire for affection. I immediately asked him to come forward and made him sit on my lap. The name of this boy was Basudev Bhattarai. He was an eight- or maybe nine-year-old from Nepal.

Eleven-year-old Sultana from Bangladesh was also among this group of children. She sat diminutively in one corner. But it seemed like the entire world could find a home in her big, deep eyes that shone with love; I was just one small individual. After some time, I called her forward too. Soon enough, I found myself plaiting her long hair like I often did for my daughter. Sultana, with her tanned skin, long face, large teeth and thick black hair, could spread the light of love and humanity with a single smile. Her voice was like that of a songbird.

During the march, I developed a very special bond with the children, particularly these two, Sultana and Basu. Upon completion of the march, they left their countries and came to stay in Delhi. My Bangladeshi daughter Sultana's story was short. She left us at a very young age. When I had met her for the first time in Manila, she didn't know a single word of Hindi. Bengali and Hindi have a lot of words in common, given that they both draw heavily from Sanskrit. To communicate better with me, Sultana had worked hard to quickly learn passable Hindi.

One day, she suddenly came up from behind and covered my eyes with her tiny hands and asked, 'Uncle, guess who?'

'These don't feel like Sultana's hands. They feel like someone else's,' I teased her.

'You don't even recognize your daughter's hands!' she said, pulling at my hair and beard.

I turned around and saw her standing there, her big eyes filled with bigger tears. I hugged and comforted her; only then did she stop crying.

She then came next to me during dinner and said softly in my ear, 'I love you more than my father, and I know you love me as much too! But you don't show it because you don't want everyone to get annoyed with me. Am I not right?'

She had another interesting way to show her affection. Everyone would march on the streets during the day, chanting slogans and making speeches at various gatherings. In the evenings, I would sit with all the children, and we would have fun just talking and sharing stories. Sultana would often get up in the middle of it and start stroking my hair. And if I tried to stop her, she would give me an exasperated look and say, 'Uncle, I know you must be exhausted after a long day of work.' I would then give her a gentle pat on the cheek to signal her to stop. But she would place her hand on my head whenever she got the chance, even if for a brief moment. She shared with me once that someone had told her when she was a child that doing this brings the blessings of angels.

Sultana's mother was her father's second wife, possibly third. She was likely half her husband's age. Her father had previously made a living as a rickshaw driver, but due to old age and illness he had become bedridden. She had an elder brother too, but he was an idler. To sustain their family, her mother and she had to work as domestic help in other people's households. There would often be days when they would have to go hungry. A social organization in Dhaka, the capital of Bangladesh, educated Sultana on a part-time basis, and provided her with additional financial assistance. The same organization had chosen her to take part in the Global March Against Child Labour. An employee of theirs had shared with us that if the girl had not received assistance in time, she could have been forced into prostitution. He mentioned that her father was suspicious of his wife's behaviour, as she would often go out dressed in new clothes.

Our global march stopped in Delhi for three days as we passed through India. Many of the girls who were participating in the march, Sultana among them, came from other countries. They were all staying in our house with my wife and me, but Sultana would act as if it was her own home, which we found endearing. At the time of leaving, she told us she would come back soon. We assumed it was just a joke.

It was the year 2001 when Sultana and her mother suddenly arrived in Delhi. They made their way straight to Mukti Ashram, picked a room and made it their own. Sultana had brought all her belongings with her. Some time back, in a similar manner, Basu had run away from Nepal and come to me. I was happy to see him, though not as surprised as I was at the arrival of Sultana. But I was more worried than surprised. The borders between Nepal and India are open, and citizens can travel freely to and from. There are several buses that operate cross-border.

For Bangladesh, however, a visa must be obtained, and the visitor must go back within the specified period. Sultana, of course, had not come here to go back.

Her father had passed away a few months after the march. She had wanted to come and stay with us ever since. Eventually, with the help of the organization which had helped with her education, she and her mother somehow reached Kolkata, in the bordering Indian state of West Bengal. They had no money for the onward journey. They were also carrying with them all their belongings and household items in four large bags and numerous smaller ones. But Sultana's mother was a clever and resourceful woman. There was no language barrier in Kolkata and so she quickly found a job as a daily wage labourer, staying there for almost a month to save money to make their way to Delhi.

They stayed at Mukti Ashram for several weeks, and even at our house for a few days. Sultana's mother felt that she and her daughter could settle in India, like many other Bangladeshis had done. We repeatedly explained to them that this would be an illegal act, but she remained insistent. We could of course not keep them with us nor advise them to stay in India even for a day after the visa expired. With great difficulty, we managed to convince them to return to Bangladesh. We knew that sending them back to Dhaka meant pushing them into a life of starvation and poverty. We had a phone conversation with the officials of the said organization there to help Sultana's elder brother before sending them back.

After the father's death, the brother had come to the realization that he would need to start earning. When I spoke to him, he mentioned that he knew how to drive an auto rickshaw. If an auto rickshaw could be arranged, it could help sustain the family. I made him promise on the Holy Quran that he would take care of Sultana and also make sure she finished her education. We then managed to arrange for a sum of forty thousand rupees (about 500 USD) for an auto rickshaw. Members of the Bangladeshi organization too promised to provide some assistance to Sultana.

That girl trusted me completely. But there was a border between India and Bangladesh, which neither her faith in me nor my capacity to keep her here could defy. I consulted lawyers and experts in an effort to make it possible to bring her back, with little success. I could not help but feel powerless.

It saddens me to see how we have created artificial distances and differences between ourselves by drawing borders on this one planet that has been given to us. The oneness of the human race can be the only true basis of civilization. Division is a sign of primitiveness and ignorance.

A few years later, Sultana's mother passed away. Later, her elder brother got her married to someone. She never came back to her house after marriage. We eventually learnt that her husband had killed her and secretly buried her. I tried to find out more from some friends in Bangladesh, but it was too late. And with the border in between, I was unable to do much else.

In the absence of similar border restrictions, Basu had a different experience. He became my friend in no time. Basu would be bursting with enthusiasm whenever he told me his story. He could often be found jumping around like an excited baby monkey. Sometimes he would climb up my shoulders or head. But he was very mindful of his health and diet, always making sure to make informed choices.

'Have you eaten?' I used to ask Basudev Bhattarai every now and then.

'Yes, Uncle, I have eaten! I have eaten a lot!' he would always respond with a smile.

At around nine, Basu appeared at most five or six years old due to his small stature. Throughout the march, I would always find him standing at the front of the stage, listening intently to the words of the speakers and taking in all the knowledge they had to offer. He told me that he wanted to be an actor when he grew up.

Basu believed that his father was a Bengali Indian and his mother was likely Nepalese. He had no idea where he was born. Though he had some faint memories of his time with his father, the rest was likely his imagination. He was very young when his father passed away and he had never met any other relatives afterwards. I believe he was born in Kathmandu, the capital of Nepal.

Kathmandu is a beautiful city, but there is just as much filth in it, much like any city anywhere else. Set in a Himalayan valley, the city is a popular destination for tourists. And the pace of life in it is dictated by the businesses that thrive on them—hotels, restaurants, bars, prostitution, entertainment and gambling. Kathmandu is also a city of historic temples, the most renowned being the ancient Pashupatinath temple of Lord Shiva. The temples and streets of Kathmandu are a shelter for thousands of children. Basu's life continues to resemble the streets he lived in—winding and crooked, undulating, narrow at some places, wide at others, some dark and closed off, and some completely open and bright. The shrieks of the buffaloes and goats being sacrificed in the temples, the lighted lamps during evening prayer, the melodious chants, the ringing of bells, drums and conch shells; the sound of cars speeding on roads and rickshaws crawling through the streets, all these have shaped his personality.

After the Global March had concluded, all of us returned to our respective countries. Basu too had gone back to Nepal. One day in January 1999, I suddenly received a call from him. I was happy to hear from him and asked him how he was.

'Uncle, wait a bit,' he replied. 'I'll come and tell you how I'm doing.'

Saying this, he abruptly hung up the phone, leaving me confused. Much to my surprise and delight, he showed up at our office a few days later. I had always suspected that he wouldn't be able to stay in Kathmandu for long.

Basu told me that when he returned to Nepal, he used the money he had saved from his daily allowance during the Global March and bought himself an old bicycle.

'But I really missed you,' he said. 'And I wanted to be with you. So, one day, I sold my bicycle and used the money to buy some clothes. With what was left, I purchased a bus ticket to Gorakhpur (a small city in northern India). Unfortunately, I didn't have enough money to make it all the way to Delhi. So, I began working at a tea shop there. I soon realized that I would have to wait for a fairly long time to receive my wages. I knew I had to act. As soon as I got a chance, I took out the exact amount of money from the counter that was necessary to reach Delhi and ran away. Uncle, I swear, I had no other intention than to reach Delhi. Now I've come to Delhi to stay.'

I didn't speak to Basu that day about right and wrong, or the immorality of stealing. I didn't yell at him for taking something without permission. But I did, later, gently impress upon him why stealing was wrong, no matter how dire the need.

He stayed with our family for a few days, giving him the time to mentally prepare for his new life at the Mukti Ashram with the other children. There, a new chapter of his life began. He was admitted to a school in Natthupura village, near the Ashram in Delhi. He would beam with pride when he talked about school.

'The day I started school was the happiest day of my life. For the first time, I felt like I was not an orphaned street child or a child labourer, but a respectable student like the other children who go to school.'

His hobbies included acting, martial arts, body building and learning the English language. He also enjoyed wearing stylish shoes, fancy dark sunglasses and fashionable clothing. He did not seem as interested in his studies though. His aspirations were grand. The Ashram staff and children often complained that he spoke to them condescendingly because of his knowledge of English. He did act selfishly at times, not bothered about others' feelings, and viewed everyone with suspicion, keeping a close eye on their shortcomings and mistakes. Basu frequently argued with his teachers too, aside from quarrelling with friends. I kept trying to explain to the children how there was a fundamental difference between how Basu saw life and how the others did. How could he escape the effects of the conditions that his childhood was spent in? The mind of a child who spent his life on the streets works differently from that of a child who spent his early life in slavery.

Basu once told me about the death of his father. 'When I called out to him for the last time,' he said, 'he didn't respond. His eyes were closed, and he didn't move. There were many people from the neighbourhood standing around him, mourning. Someone told me that my father had passed away. But I couldn't believe it. He was right in front of me. I started to cry, so people removed me from there and took him away. I don't know where they took him. After that day, I never saw my father. My acquaintances helped me for a few days, but eventually all of them abandoned me. One day, the landlord asked me to vacate the house. I was really sad that day. I used to look for my father in everything I saw in the house. The bed on which he used to tell stories from his life and give advice, the floor of the room and the verandah where he used to play with me, the door through which he carried me out in his arms. All these things were very dear to me. I could see my father's smiling face in everything. Leaving that house meant leaving my father again. I didn't know where I was going.'

Hungry and parched, he went out to beg in the evening. Stretching his arms out to beg for the first time, he said, felt akin to slicing his own throat to kill himself. Some people gave him money or food out of pity, while others showered him with abuses. What he was most concerned about that day, however, was where he was going to spend the night. Exhausted, he found a spot on the footpath and tried to sleep, unaware that the area was populated by gangs of street children, led by individuals who were not particularly welcoming to newcomers. Street gangs divide areas for begging among themselves as well as spots to sleep on the pavement at night. There is little choice for a new child but to accept the authority of the gang leader.

Basu lay down on the footpath without permission and was soon beaten up by a bunch of thuggish boys. It didn't take long for him to begin earning enough to feed himself. He even managed to save some money, which he would spend on good food along with other beggars. Later, his 'seniors' pushed him into taking drugs. Once he got hooked, he needed more money than before to sustain his habit, which begging could not provide. Some of the children from the footpath under the bridge where he slept would go out early in the mornings with empty sacks slung over their shoulders. He discovered that they were rag pickers who collected plastic, iron, aluminium and glass from garbage heaps, which could then be sold at varying prices. So he decided to join them.

I asked him how long he worked as a rag picker, and why he decided to stop doing that work.

'A companion of mine introduced me to his friend,' he said. 'He used to pickpocket. At first, I refused to do it. It felt wrong. One day, I found I had no money left. I couldn't buy food, or drugs. So when I saw an opportunity, I took it and picked a man's pocket. I got lucky that day. That first wallet I picked was full of money. We really enjoyed ourselves. We ate lots of chicken, smoked some nice cigarettes, and just generally had fun. It felt like I was born to do this.'

He soon became a masterful pickpocket. His innocent face and small stature certainly helped. One night, his entourage was at the airport in Kathmandu, waiting for flights to arrive late in the evening. The passengers began to depart hauling their luggage away on trolleys, when Basu, who had been lying in wait, suddenly snatched a small briefcase from one of the trolleys and ran, actually managing to flee with it. When he and his companions were at a safe distance, they opened the briefcase and were ecstatic to find many bundles of notes inside. But their joy was short-lived. One of the boys identified them to be fake currency notes.

They sat around hurling insults at those involved in the business of counterfeit money that night. Feeling miserably cold, they began burning the bundles one by one, using the fire to warm their hands and feet. Suddenly, one of their companions arrived at the scene, and shouted out in alarm, seeing the bundles of notes being set ablaze, 'What have you done, you fool!' He quickly grabbed two bundles out of the flame. One was partially burned, while the other was still undamaged.

'You fools,' he said, 'you are burning the IC [Indian currency]! These are even more valuable than NC [Nepalese currency]!'

Basu cursed himself for his stupidity. The next morning, as soon as the shops opened, all of them first went to a nice restaurant and ate the costliest food. They then bought nice shoes, clothes, belts and glasses. The next couple days went by in such indiscriminate self-indulgence. So much so, that they had spent all the money before the third.

The following months were a struggle, spent doing odd jobs to make ends meet. However, Basu's life changed when he was taken to Balgriha, a residential centre for street children, run by an organization called CWIN (Child Workers in Nepal) in Kathmandu. He was happy to be there.

Balgriha also had a teacher for imparting basic education to the children. One day, the teacher asked the children to recite the alphabet, which had been written out on the blackboard. When Basu repeatedly failed to do as he was instructed, she became enraged and hurled the wooden duster at him. Infuriated, he ran into the kitchen and came back with a large knife, with which he lunged at the woman, attempting to stab her in the stomach. Fortunately, she managed to escape. The elder boys then beat him severely. But Basu was not expelled. Instead, the institution focused on helping him improve his behaviour.

Basu and I would often converse like friends. One day, he began to reminisce about his first love.

'Do you want to know, Uncle, how I realized that I had fallen in love with my teacher?'

'Yes, do tell.'

'There was a beautiful young woman in our organization who used to come and teach English to children as part of her social service,' Basu recalled. 'She also occasionally did some modelling on television. The first day she saw me and asked, "Who is this little stud?" I felt very shy to be referred to as a "stud".'

'How old were you then?' I asked him.

'Eight.'

He continued, 'One day, we children were watching television, and she came on. When some of them started making fun of the way our teacher was acting, I got so angry that I thrashed them.'

'So, did your teacher find out about this?'

'No, but my friends told me that this is what real love feels like. I was really falling for her. I had even started to dream about getting married to her.'

'Then what happened?' I asked, laughing, but genuinely eager to know.

'What was bound to happen! One evening, I noticed that a farewell ceremony for the teacher was being held in the meeting room. All the children and staff had gathered there. I hid behind the bathroom, crying. My friends knew that I couldn't bear to be separated from her. Two or three older boys came to me. They warned me that this was the perfect chance to show my love. "Don't let it slip away, or else you'll regret it for the rest of your days," they said.'

'What did you do then?' I asked, unable to contain my curiosity.

'I listened to them. I plucked a rose from a pot and stood behind the stage. But I could not find it in me to go and speak to her. I was on the brink of tears when those boys told me to show courage. I finally made it to the stage and knelt in front of her, tears streaming down my face. Madam's eyes were also filled with tears, and I could feel her affection for me. I presented her with the flower and declared my love for her. "I love you," I said to her.'

I burst into laughter. 'So, did you get married then?' I asked.

'Just like you,' he said, 'the entire room erupted in laughter when I said it. Even the teacher couldn't help but join in. Then, she called out to me and said, "Basu, you're still so young. You barely come up to my shoulder! We'll get married when you're as tall as me." She hugged and kissed me as she said this.'

Basu had completed his tenth grade while living in Mukti

Ashram. Then he got a job at a call centre. After he left that job, Basu rented a room in Burari village near the Ashram and started a small English teaching centre called 'American and British Institute of Lingua-Franca'. Many young men and women seeking better employment would come to study English at his centre. Basu was thus able to make a decent living from running it, although he had to eventually close it down due to a conflict with some local people. Subsequently, he expressed his desire to work in the Bachpan Bachao Andolan, like many of the other children who had grown up at the Ashram. Local and foreign visitors regularly come to our organization to volunteer. The staff of the organization entrusted Basu with the responsibility of organizing these youth volunteers. He took on this work, though he could not continue for very long.

It was around this time that I was invited to an international event in Rajasthan at which many distinguished people were in attendance. I had taken young Basu with me. He shared his story in one of the sessions, which left a lasting impression on all the attendees. Lewis Miranda was one of them, and he grew to be very fond of Basu. He was an entrepreneur and a renowned activist, well-versed in economic and social issues. He was also the founder of and advisor to many organizations, and he continues to provide assistance to Basu in all aspects of his life.

There are many stories of Basu's female friendships. He befriended many girls while working at the call centre, then later while teaching English, staying with foreign volunteers, on social media, or attending late night parties with friends. He used to tell me about them and even ask for my advice. Basu and I would joke a lot.

'Aunty,' he would sometimes tease Sumedha ji, 'uncle was so handsome. Many girls must have been attracted to him.' Then, before she could make a face and say something, he would add in a mischievous manner, 'Yeah, but you're also so beautiful... many boys must have fallen for you too.'

But he wouldn't stop there. 'You're getting old now...' he would tease us. 'You better accept the fact that no one's going to have a crush on you two any more.'

Basu's longing for love, fame and respect drove him to do foolish things. No matter how much money he earned, he squandered it all on his friends, who often took advantage of his generosity. I could see this, so I would keep encouraging him to get married and hopefully find some stability in life.

He and I spoke to numerous girls and their families for marriage. However, these conversations went nowhere since little was known about his family background, and he had no home or even a stable job. This caused him immense pain. He would often break down in front of me. He eventually found love in Delhi, although it wasn't easy. He confided in me that he was deeply in love with a girl and was ready to commit to her. He was confident that she reciprocated his feelings. So Sumedha ji and I called the girl to Mukti Ashram and spoke to her. It was clear that she liked him too.

The name of the girl was Chetna. She was scared to tell her family members about Basu, so, a few weeks later, we invited her parents and close relatives to join us for dinner at our place. All the old questions resurfaced once more. Basu was working with us at the time. He had also obtained a master's degree. Chetna's relatives closely scrutinized our interactions and behaviour with him. They inquired about his salary and status. Incidentally, some of Chetna's relatives knew of me and held me in high regard. Her relatives were now certain that the boy was not an orphan even though he had been separated from his parents and had lived alone since he was a child. Furthermore, we promised them that they would not have to spend any money on

Chetna's marriage, and that we would cover all the costs of the wedding. They finally agreed. Basu and Chetna were married at Mukti Ashram, a place that held many fond memories for Basu, where had spent much of his childhood and adolescence. In the presence of over two hundred people from our organization, as well as Chetna's family and friends, a grand wedding ceremony was held in accordance with Hindu customs.

Chetna was offered a job at Bachpan Bachao Andolan soon after the marriage. She kept up with her work until a few months before the birth of their daughter. Her husband was not someone who could stay in one place for an extended period of time. Once again, he had a disagreement with some of the staff of the organization.

As time went on, Basu began to understand that he needed greater knowledge, maturity and discipline for social work. So, he completed a course in Non-profit Management, and is now working diligently on a project with a non-profit organization. Chetna and he named their beautiful baby girl Alex. She brought along with her immense joy and happiness. And it appears that his daughter's love is helping Basu become a more responsible and dependable individual. He is probably also learning to temper his dreams to reality. The joy and contentment I experience when Alex calls me Dadu (paternal grandfather) on the phone, reminds me of the faith Basu reposed in me, which had motivated him to leave Nepal for Delhi.

Our Global March Against Child Labour was a success thanks to Sultana, Basu and the countless other child marchers who joined us. The children who participated in the march fondly remember with immense pride the privilege of attending the International Labour Organization's annual convention in Geneva, on the final day of the march. 'Go-Go, Global March! Stop-Stop Child

Labour!', 'No More Tools in Tiny Hands, We Want Books, We Want Toys!' the six hundred global marchers present there had chanted. The auditorium had echoed with these slogans. It was the result of the tenacity, enthusiasm and energy of the children that, within a year of the march, governments, employers' organizations and labour unions around the world responded to our demands and an international convention against the worst forms child labour was adopted. This was the first ILO convention to be ratified by every ILO member country.

Upon the Grave of a Living Friend

One end of this story is tied to the tunnels of the mica mines and death wells in the jungles of Jharkhand and Bihar, and the other to the glitz and glamour of luxury cars and fashion shows in New York, London and Paris.

It is a story, scripted by nature and then by man, of a substance, delicate and transparent yet one whose walls can withstand the strongest currents of electricity, and also trap thousands in slavery. It is also the story of a boy who broke though these walls, whose life emerges as a song from the silence born of hopelessness and helplessness. This is the story of Manan Ansari.

'Do you ever think about how your perfumes, creams, powders and other cosmetic products are made? Have you ever considered what is used to make your car shine so brightly? It's time to take a closer look at the reality behind these products. Your lives cannot run without electrical appliances and equipment. But you cannot imagine the price that is paid for the material used to make these products for you—mica. It is with the blood and sweat of thousands of children like me that mica is extracted from mines. These mica mines are graves for innumerable children and their parents, who are buried alive under them.'

This poignant and thought-provoking statement was made by thirteen-year-old Manan Ansari at a special event of the International Labour Organization in Geneva in 2009, held to mark the tenth anniversary of the adoption of the Convention on the Worst Forms of Child Labour. His words left the leaders and officials in attendance stunned.

Manan was born in the mica belt of Jharkhand. He was the seventh child in a family of five brothers and three sisters, two of whom were already married. His parents, who worked as labourers in the mines, did not have the means to provide their children with an education. So they sent the children to work in the mines to collect *dhibra* (small pieces of mica). Manan did this for two years. He still grows sad when he thinks about those days.

'We would leave in the morning with pickaxes, shovels, spades and old plastic bags,' he recalls. 'The work there was incredibly hazardous. Earthen mounds were dug at multiple spots to create large pits and ditches, which we would then enter to extract dhibra. Mica is a shiny and sharp material like glass. Each piece of dhibra had many thin layers of mica like the layers of an onion. While peeling these layers, we would end up cutting our fingers. The mica dust would sting our skin. Particularly in the summer, this mica dust would stick to our sweat and make it itch terribly. We would get multiple scratches all over the body. Our lives were worse than that of animals.'

But the trauma was not merely physical. 'I was the youngest of the children staying in the hostel of Bal Ashram,' he once told me, 'so I was given the bottom bed in the bunker cots. I used to have nightmares every night, and I would sit up in bed again and again. I would feel like I was lying inside a tunnel and picking dhibra with my hands, and that the soil was going to come crashing down on me and bury me alive.'

Two brothers, Ilyas and Imaar, who lived in Manan's neighbourhood, also used to go to the mine to dig for dhibra. They were Manan's friends. One morning, they told Manan that they wanted to finish their work early and return home since they had a family wedding to attend. Some time after, Manan suddenly heard a loud wailing coming from the other corner of the ditch they were working in, and before he could make sense of what was happening, it had caved in. While Imaar had somehow managed to escape, Ilyas had been buried alive. Imaar was screaming and sobbing. Fear overwhelmed Manan and he began to cry as well. The two boys began frantically calling out for Ilyas while running around inside the tunnel to figure out where he was. Some labourers working nearby rushed to the spot where the noise was coming from. They were horrified too. The mine that was meant to provide Ilyas with a living had become his grave. Manan was in shock. But fear and sadness do not satisfy hunger. On the following day, life returned to its usual routine. The labourers picked up their shovels and hoes and went to work in the mines. Everything was as it had been except for the absence of his friend, Ilyas. Ilyas and Imaar's mother had died in a nearby mine the same way a year previously.

India is the largest producer of mica in the world, accounting for around sixty per cent of the global supply. This mineral is mainly found in the eastern region of north India, particularly the Giridih and Koderma districts of Jharkhand and Nawada district of Bihar. Ground mica is used in the production of cosmetics as its shiny powder adds a unique texture to them. The same quality also lends itself to the manufacture of pearlescent paints for automobiles. But mica has excellent electrical resistance too. The thin and transparent sheets of mica are remarkably effective in blocking the flow of electricity. It is also known for its heat-insulating properties, as it does not melt or burn easily at high temperatures. This makes it an ideal substance for insulation in small and large electrical transformers, switches, irons, toasters and heaters. Mica is also used in rockets and missiles.

Mica extraction is a major source of livelihood for hundreds of thousands of people in approximately two hundred and fifty villages of Koderma, Giridih and Nawada districts. Many of the people belong to the various tribes that live in this region. These areas lag far behind much of the country in terms of development, and a lot of the non-forested land being barren and uncultivable making farming impossible, large numbers are forced into mining. Additionally, Maoism has been a major issue in the area, with frequent clashes between Maoist fighters and the police being reported. Moving through these parts after sunset can be risky. There are police checkpoints at various locations here.

Out of the approximately five thousand children involved in the extraction of mica, many of them are as young as five to six years. Most of the villages lack schools and the ones that do exist are barely functional. Local traders and contractor labourers will purchase dhibra at a rate of Rs 2–3 per kilogram. An adult man can extract an average of ten to twelve kilos of dhibra per day, sometimes less. The financial condition of the dhibra pickers is thus very poor. What is more, many people in the area are prone to serious diseases like tuberculosis from inhaling the dhibra dust.

Manan is from a village called Shamsihariya. I have been there twice. In those days, the village had no electricity and no hospital. It did have a school where classes were taught up to the fifth grade; there were only two teachers though. One can only imagine how these two teachers must have managed the five grades. A student who wished to pursue further education had to travel to the Domchanch village school, which was located eighteen kilometres away. The 'Mica Field' bus was a lifeline for the labourers of Shamsihariya, leaving at around eight in the morning to take them to the mines and returning late in the evening. It was also a vital means of communication with the other villages in the area. It was this bus they took to go get medicine when sick, send their children to school, run around for marriage preparations or to visit their kin for social functions or in the case of death. If the bus ever stopped plying, it meant that everything had come to a standstill.

But their problems did not end there. Manan once recounted a custom in his village.

'All households had to take turns to send one of their members to go out of the village to collect funds for the Jamaat [religious assembly in the Muslim community]. When I was around six or seven years old,' he said, 'it was my father's turn to go. My two elder brothers had to go out each day to collect dhibra. My mother and elder brother were ill, but my father was still expected to leave the house for a month to collect donations for the Jamaat.'

'Did he still have to go?' I asked with curiosity.

'Yes,' he said. 'We made numerous requests to the organizers, but we were unable to prevent my father from leaving.'

'What happened to your family after that?'

'The people of the community assured us that they would take care of us. They did send some food a couple of times, but that's it. We all but starved to death. I was very angry at all of them. We were already upset about my father's absence, and on top of that, we were unable to sleep at night because of hunger. It was dadagiri in the name of religion!'

During those difficult days, Manan once spotted a boy from the neighbourhood tending to a flock of goats. He asked the boy if he had to go hungry too. The boy told him he didn't; he used to get some money for grazing other people's goats. Inspired by what he had found out, Manan went to his uncle who had some goats. He took a milch goat from his uncle, which he then began taking out for grazing. Along with the goat came her recently born lamb. Manan developed a deep affection for the lamb. He would make him sleep on the bed beside him, and during the cold winter nights, he would drape his blanket over him to keep him warm.

'What happened to the goat and the lamb then?' I asked him.

'That lamb was dearer to me than my younger brother,' he said. 'But he was soon separated from me.'

'Did he get lost? Or did he die?'

'No, no! That's not what happened,' he replied woefully. 'My mother had me sleep away from the lamb one night, making up some excuse. I had no idea that I'd never see him again. If I had known, I'd have held him close that night,' his voice choking as he said this. 'When I woke up in the morning, I went to the verandah to see the lamb, but it was nowhere to be found. I began to cry. My mother then told me that a snake had bit the lamb and it had died. I cried all day. I used to eat only after feeding a piece of bread to it. Every evening when I returned with its mother, that beautiful black lamb would cuddle up to her and jump around with joy. It would feed at her teats, and then jump up and try to nibble at my cheeks, nose, ears or my fingers.'

The truth was that Manan's mother had had to sell the lamb to a neighbour for some money. He only found out many days later.

The boy's mind had begun to explore the complexities of life, and for days afterwards he felt overwhelmed by the dilemma with which he was faced. He loved the little lamb, and couldn't help but acknowledge the sad fact that his mother had selfishly taken an innocent child away from its mother to feed her own children. He felt rage, but he had sympathy for his mother at the same time.

Manan also used to practise running on the sandy shores near the village pond. He ran faster than any of the other children, including another child, Bilal, who used to run there too. He was slightly older than Manan, and a bit more stout. One day, Bilal beat up Manan, leaving him feeling humiliated and powerless. Manan quietly went home but was determined on getting even. He continued to strengthen his arms and legs, exercising his muscles by leaning against trees or walls, and beat Bilal up badly the very next chance he got to fight him. His family was upset with his actions, and punished him by relieving him of the task of grazing goats and instead sent him to collect mica along with his elder brother and sister from the very next day.

His trip to Geneva was a contrast to the grim reality of his early childhood. We got off the plane and went through immigration at the airport. From there, we made our way to the train station. I had been to Geneva multiple times before, so I was aware that there were direct trains to the city. Manan suddenly expressed his need to use the restroom, and he quickly ran to the urinal. Unfortunately, he returned just a few seconds too late, and the train had already departed. He was taken aback to discover that there are places in the world where trains run not by the hour or minute, but by the second. He regretted missing the train, but also learnt a valuable lesson.

He had come to attend an International Labour Organization programme in Geneva. Child labourers from all over the world spoke passionately about their experiences of suffering, exploitation and liberation and about hope and change. They served as a beacon of hope, emphasizing that poverty should never be used as an excuse to take away someone's childhood. It is the responsibility of the governments to ensure freedom, respect and education to every child. To turn away from this responsibility or to make excuses is a crime against humanity. He appealed for a boycott of any beauty product whose shine was created through the blood and sweat of children like him.

We stayed in a hostel at a training centre for Christian missionaries in Geneva. There, he discovered for the first time that there were many sects among Christians, each with their own churches.

'I used to think only Hindus and Muslims had different sects,' he asked me with great surprise. 'Is there so much division among Christians too? Why does this happen? Don't the followers get confused?'

I explained to him that there was nothing wrong in reaching the same destination by taking different routes. That one only ought to have the freedom to choose whichever path one prefers. Problems arise when one tries to belittle the other's path by asserting that their way is the only, or the best, way. I told him that this had been the nature of most conflict throughout history, and that though we may strive to find the truth, or God, through our intellect, with science and logic, we should not look at those who have taken different paths with disdain.

Manan's biggest problem in Geneva was the lack of spicy Indian food. After the programme ended, we went to an Indian restaurant for lunch. While he enjoyed his meal there, he was angry about the fact that the water was not complimentary and that we had to purchase a bottle to drink. He grumbled for a while. After that, we went for a stroll along the renowned Lake Geneva. He was astonished to see the stunning, vibrant lights twinkling on both sides.

'Look, Bhai Sahab ji,' he exclaimed in awe as he saw the fountains and colourful lights in the middle of the lake, 'it's like many rainbows are diving into the lake all at once!'

'Let's go touch the rainbows and come back!' I suggested.

He was ecstatic and we hopped on a boat ride across the lake. The view was breathtaking, with the vibrant fountains and a picturesque skyline. We disembarked at the other side and strolled towards the old city.

'It's amazing how clean the water and the bank is here,' he remarked. 'There's also a great deal of security in place. I've heard that the wealthy from all over the world keep their illicit funds in Swiss banks, which explains why there are so many grand and impressive banks on every street. A lot of money from the wealthy of our country will be deposited here somewhere. If the funds are returned to our nation, arrangements can be made for the education and healthcare of hundreds of thousands of children like me.'

I only patted him on the back.

There was another cheap restaurant in the area I knew of, which claimed to be an Indian restaurant but was in fact a

Bangladeshi one. We went there too. After that, we crossed the bridge on foot and returned to our hostel, marvelling at the beautiful buildings that surrounded the lake. It was a stunning sight, with the palatial structures on all three sides of it illuminated with glittering, colourful lights.

After Shamsihariya was selected to be made into a Bal Mitra Gram (child-friendly village), the work began of enrolling children in school and taking them out of manual labour. Our friends managed to persuade Manan's father, but the bigger challenge was the jamadar, who oversaw the mining work, from whom he had taken an advance. The activists threatened to take legal action against the jamadar, and only then were the fifteen children working at the mine freed. Manan was brought to Bal Ashram in 2008, along with the fourteen other children, as his family could not afford to educate him.

For several days after he joined, he remained jittery and suspicious, which is common for new children. However, there was something different in his case. One day, he shared his confusion with an older Muslim child already living there.

'All the children living here are poor. We are just like them, but most of them are Hindus. How can we live with them?'

'At first, I thought the same way,' the child explained. 'But back then I used to think like my family and our local maulvi. These people, instead of showing me love, forced me to work in a welding workshop. That workshop belonged to an uncle of the maulvi. Bal Ashram not only gave me a home and an education, it also taught me to live with respect and love.'

'I don't agree with that,' Manan said, and with that, he stopped talking to the boy.

Manan's village had around fifty to sixty households. All the inhabitants were Muslim and relied on mica mining for their livelihood in addition to a few other trades that could earn them a small income like poultry farming and goat rearing. Some fundamentalist mullahs used to visit the village now and then to preach their narrow-minded beliefs, and unfortunately, they had had a profound effect on Manan's father and other family members. Upon arriving at the Ashram, he initially attempted to foster a friendship with only the Muslim children. It seemed natural to him that instead of being friends with Hindu children the other Muslim children too would prefer those of their own community. And what is more, he felt that the Hindu and Christian children would themselves not want to be his friends either. It was difficult for him to understand why there was no discrimination among the children at the Ashram. What caused Manan further distress was the fact that some of the children who had been rescued with him quickly began to mix with the others. He kept trying to convince them, and when they refused to listen, he resorted to fighting with them.

One Sunday, Sumedha ji and I, and everyone at the Ashram, young and old, were celebrating the birthdays of some of the children. The children who come to us often don't know their birthdays. And so, to strengthen their sense of identity and instil greater self-respect in them, we pick a holiday to celebrate birthdays for several children at a time. That day, after we were done celebrating, I asked the Hindu children sitting there to raise their hands. Three or four newly arrived children in the Ashram responded. Likewise, when it was the turn of the Muslim children, all the new children raised their hands, with Manan being the first to do so. In each case, they sat with their arms raised, looking around in confusion, as none of the sixty-odd kids present, who had been staying here for some time, had joined them.

I asked Puran Banjara, an old student, to get up and ask the Hindu and Muslim children to differentiate between their religions. He made one child from each group stand up and asked them to speak on behalf of their respective communities.

'How many legs does a Hindu child have? How many legs does a Muslim child have?' Puran asked the children.

'Two,' they replied.

'How many hands does a Hindu child have? How many hands does a Muslim child have?' he went on.

'Two,' they said once again.

He then asked them to count their hands, feet, nose, ears, et cetera again. The children looked on curiously, moving their hands back and forth as they counted.

'Why do children of all religions have two eyes, two ears, two hands, two legs, one nose, one head, and one mouth?' Puran asked. 'If Bhagwan or Allah were different, wouldn't Hindus and Muslims have different numbers of hands, legs, heads, ears or eyes?' After this, he insisted, 'Come! Let us get a blood test done. It may be that the blood of a child who identifies as Muslim may be green and that of a Hindu may be yellow, white, or any other colour.'

'No!' all the children said together. 'We know very well that our blood is red.' They became a bit anxious for a moment.

'Can a Hindu survive without air, water or food?' Puran asked.

'No,' everyone replied in unison.

'Can a Muslim live without air, water or food?' he then asked.

Once again, the answer was a resounding 'No'. Some children had started smiling now though others were still a little hesitant. But eventually, they all agreed that they were all humans. Manan remembers that incident as the biggest lesson of his life. He was content in the belief that the children in the Ashram had absolute liberty to pray and worship in their own manner.

After a few more years, Manan had memorized many mantras from the Vedas advocating for humanity, justice, equality and environmental conservation, which many people found hard to believe. He could tell you about the practice of fasting during Ramadan and offering namaz as lucidly as he could explain the rituals involved in a yagya.

'I often look back on those days with a mix of amusement and embarrassment,' he now says with a chuckle. 'While living in Bal Ashram, we realized that there was hardly any place in the world where people of all religions, castes and social classes could live together without discrimination. It took me a while to understand that our fraternity was only a fraternity of human beings, regardless of our religion, caste or social status. Discrimination based on these factors is nothing but a conspiracy spread by those who seek to divide us and maintain their power.'

After studying in the Ashram for a few months, he was enrolled at a government school in a nearby village. He achieved remarkable success by scoring eighty per cent marks in his sixth grade examination and stood first in the class. Sumedha ji rewarded him with a watch, which further boosted his enthusiasm for studies. In fact, from then on until the ninth grade, Manan always topped his class. He was an exceptional player of badminton, volleyball and cricket, and was always enthusiastic about participating in plays, singing and other cultural programmes. He won numerous awards in debate, writing, singing and general knowledge competitions. Once, he came third in a national-level singing competition held in Delhi. For a few years in the beginning, he dreamed of becoming a doctor, since there was no qualified doctor, or even a good dispensary, in his or any of the surrounding villages. Then, by the time he reached the eleventh grade, he began to consider becoming a scientist. He did very well in his twelfth grade examinations.

Sumedha ji has been trained in classical music for many years. She always takes out time to practise and polish her skills, and when she stays at the Bal Ashram, she also teaches children who are interested in music. Manan Ansari, Imtiaz, Veeru, Suraj and Asmit used to gather around her whenever she was there to learn from her. Back in his village in Bihar, Imtiaz's maternal uncle was renowned for singing qawwalis. The young boy had a beautiful voice and was quite good at singing. It didn't take him as long to learn music from Sumedha ji as other children. Then there was Manan, who, despite his best efforts, could not help his nasal voice. To help him, Sumedha ji would guide him to sing the melody while holding his nose. He regards her as not merely his teacher but also as his mother. He was an incredibly hardworking child, and he eventually improved his singing, working on it by waking up at three or four in the morning and practising for hours.

When I stay at the Bal Ashram, I often take strolls around the playground in the mornings or evenings. The children await my arrival, and as soon as they see me, they rush up to me and give me a hug. We then chat like old friends, discussing topics like home, family, the Ashram, life in general, the country and the world. It also gives them an opportunity to air their grievances. But they are a curious bunch, and always come prepared with their lists of questions. Manan used to ask me a lot of questions too. He would often ask me about politics, science and technology.

I think this happened when he was in the eleventh or twelfth standard. I had been noticing for some days in these gatherings that Manan was starting to dress up more than usual. It didn't take me long to notice his shiny shoes, his shirt tucked neatly into his trousers, dark sunglasses on his eyes, and his hair slicked back with oil. It was clear that our little brother was growing up.

'Mian, you're looking cheerful!' I said to him one day, when the two of us were alone. 'What's the matter?'

'No, Bhai Sahab ji,' he said, blushing. 'It's nothing.'

'Be honest with me, big man,' I said. 'Is there a girl you've become friends with? Don't try to hide it.'

He blushed some more and then spoke slowly, 'I'm not sure why, but there's a girl in my class who keeps smiling at me with a certain look in her eyes. She's very good at studies and excels in singing competitions also.' Then, as we walked, he took a few steps back from me and, not meeting my gaze, said, 'It seems she has fallen in love with me after hearing me sing. Once, I defeated her in a singing competition, but she still came over to congratulate me. She said, "Manan, you sing really well," and ever since then, I've been feeling something inside.'

Before I could say something, however, in the form of advice about teenage love and mutual attraction, he said, 'But I don't want to get involved in this. I need to focus on my studies. It's nice to be dressed well, though.'

A few months later, he informed me that the girl had moved to a private school for her twelfth grade studies. They had not seen each other since then. Manan was aware of the importance of the twelfth grade board exams, and understood the significant impact it had on one's future. It was no wonder that everything else was relegated to the background as he kept himself busy with his studies, often late into the night.

Manan was deeply moved and greatly influenced by the story of Suman Mahto, a child from Bihar. His widowed mother worked as a domestic help in Saharsa, a city in eastern Bihar. When she fell sick, she borrowed money from her employer and sent her eight-year-old son, Suman, to work in her place. Fortunately, our organization was able to rescue him. Suman was an introverted child and a good student. He was an exceptionally talented painter and writer, and also a skilled volleyball and cricket player. His dream was to become an engineer. However, he was unable to secure admission due to poor performance in the twelfth grade. Having identified his interests and talents, we encouraged him to pursue a course in computer graphics design, and in 2013, he enrolled at a renowned institution in Delhi. He successfully completed that course in 2014 and went on to get another diploma in design.

Suman initially began his career as a graphic designer in a corporate setting, and then in the Bachpan Bachao Andolan. But he soon realized that it wasn't the right fit for him. He had been very passionate about yoga ever since he was a child and had become highly skilled in yogasanas during his time in the Ashram. Alongside his college education in Delhi, he had completed a diploma in Yoga Vidya from a reputed yoga institute. Manan had enrolled at Delhi University around this time. He got into microbiology, as he had wanted to.

Manan and Suman became good friends and moved in together to a small house that we had rented close to our own for the two boys. Manan soon began attending a renowned music college. Despite their bond, though, Manan never did yoga, nor did Suman accompany him in his singing. Of course, both often used to go to Sumedha ji to complain about each other's lack of contribution to chores such as cooking, washing dishes or cleaning the house!

Manan, along with some of his college mates, had formed a small band in which he sang and his friends played the piano and tabla. During his free time or on holidays, he would come to our place and practise with Sumedha ji. He would return to his room and practise until midnight if she ever expressed her dissatisfaction with his singing. His eagerness to learn, humility and reverence for his teacher earned him numerous awards at the university for singing. He became incredibly popular among the students, and some of the girls were even quite fond of him. But Manan was focused on his studies, and none of these friendships ever went beyond the strictly platonic.

Once, Sumedha ji received a call from Manan around midnight. He sounded very anxious.

'Mother, I've been getting some strange messages on my phone for a few days now,' he told her. 'I thought they were random messages, so I didn't tell you. Someone wanted to talk to me on the phone this evening, and then the man started insisting that we meet. Just a while back, I received several calls from unknown numbers, which I immediately disconnected. I'm a bit scared and uneasy... Can I come and meet you?'

'Why do you even need to ask?' Sumedha ji replied.

He arrived a few minutes later, and what he showed her deeply shocked and worried her. His phone contained short videos, photos and stories inciting hatred against Islam, claiming that Muslims had committed untold atrocities. The phone numbers had area codes of foreign countries and were likely fake.

Sumedha ji carefully observed the videos and realized that they showed the atrocities of the Islamic State on Yezidi Muslims in Syria but were being presented as if they were incidents from Kashmir and other parts of India. She hugged Manan and told him there was nothing to fear, and that if he received such messages in future, or was harassed, they would approach the police. He had his exams in a few days, so he deleted all the contents from his phone and turned it off. Suman had a spare phone for emergency use.

After completing his bachelor's from Delhi University, in 2018, Manan got admission in a renowned university in Odisha to pursue an MSc degree. I was told that he had got into a romantic relationship with a girl studying at the university.

Manan attended the Laureates and Leaders for Children Summit in Jordan that same year and delivered a speech emphasizing the importance of safeguarding the rights of children for global peace. He also accompanied us to a refugee camp in Syria, where he met many children and heard the harrowing stories of the atrocities they had endured. He was outraged at these violent acts committed in the name of religion. In 2019, he was invited to the International Conference on 'Business and Human Rights' in Geneva, where he discussed the success of Bal Mitra Grams as an effective way of providing freedom, education and security to children. He explained in detail how child labour and trafficking have been eliminated from the supply chains of domestic and foreign companies by transforming settlements in the mica region into child-friendly villages, in addition to ending child marriage and illiteracy.

He was himself amazed by the transformation that had taken place when he visited his village.

'Now all the kids in my village are attending school!' he exclaimed with joy on his last trip home. 'Even the girls are riding bicycles to get there! The village school offers classes up to the tenth grade. My younger sister has completed her bachelor's degree and is now married. Many of the children in the village attend English-medium schools.' He then added, hesitant but proud, 'Bhai Sahab ji, when I go to the village, the whole village surrounds me. People used to respect me before, thinking I was special to you, but now they consider me something even more special. Not only in my village, but the children of many nearby villages look to me as a role model.'

Manan is indeed a role model for countless children. In 2020, he finished his master's degree with excellent marks. He is currently employed as a junior scientist at an international institute and is striving to gain admission to a prestigious institute in Europe or America to pursue research in microbiology. We are certain that he will go on to distinguish himself in his chosen discipline. He is a determined individual. 'Even child labourers have the capacity to achieve greatness,' he always believed.